PROTECTING INDIVIDUAL PRIVACY

IN EVALUATION RESEARCH

The Committee on Federal Agency Evaluation Research
Assembly of Behavioral and Social Sciences
National Research Council

National Academy of Sciences
Washington, D.C.

1975

```
JC
599
.U5
N35
1975
```

NOTICE

The members of the committee appointed to undertake the study reported here were chosen on the basis of recognized competence and with due consideration for a balance of disciplines and expertise appropriate to the project. Responsibility for the content of this report rests with that committee.

The project was approved by the Governing Board of the National Research Council, representing and consisting of members of the National Academy of Sciences, the National Academy of Engineering, and the Institute of Medicine.

Each report of a committee of the National Research Council is reviewed by an independent group according to procedures established and monitored by a Report Review Committee representing and consisting of members of the National Academy of Sciences, the National Academy of Engineering, and the Institute of Medicine.

International Standard Book No. ISBN 0-309-02406-4

Library of Congress Catalog Card No. 75-18591

Available from:

Printing and Publishing Office
National Academy of Sciences
2101 Constitution Avenue, N.W.
Washington, D.C. 20418

Printed in the United States of America

COMMITTEE ON FEDERAL AGENCY EVALUATION RESEARCH

Members

Alice M. Rivlin, (CHAIRMAN), Senior Fellow, Brookings Institution, Washington, DC[*]

Donald T. Campbell, Professor of Psychology, Northwestern University

James Farmer, President, Council on Minority Planning and Strategy, Washington, DC

Robinson G. Hollister, Jr., Professor of Economics, Swarthmore College

Robert A. Levine, President, New York City RAND Institute[#]

Paul A. Nejelski, Director, Institute of Judicial Administration, New York University

Martin Rein, Professor of Urban Studies and Planning, Massachusetts Institute of Technology

Peter H. Rossi, Chairman, Department of Social Relations, Johns Hopkins University[o]

Richard D. Schwartz, Provost and Dean of Faculty of Law and Jurisprudence, Law School, State University of New York

Joseph Steinberg, Assistant Commissioner for Office of Survey Design, Bureau of Labor Statistics, U.S. Department of Labor[+]

John F. Szwed, Director, Center for Urban Ethnography, University of Pennsylvania

Sheldon H. White, Professor of Psychology, Harvard University

The Committee is grateful to Stephen S. Baratz, who served as Executive Secretary for most of the Committee's life, and to Marsha Paller and Theodore Voorhees, Jr., who provided valuable research assistance at an early stage of the Committee's deliberations.

---

[*]Now, Director, Congressional Budget Office
[#]Now, Deputy Director, Congressional Budget Office
[o]Now, Professor of Sociology, University of Massachusetts
[+]Now, President, Survey Design, Inc., Silver Spring, MD

PROTECTING INDIVIDUAL PRIVACY IN EVALUATION RESEARCH

TABLE OF CONTENTS

SUMMARY AND RECOMMENDATIONS   1

THE NEED FOR PROTECTING INDIVIDUAL PRIVACY
IN EVALUATION RESEARCH   3

    Background of the Committee on Federal
      Agency Evaluation Research
    The Need for Evaluation
    Protection of Privacy
    Findings and Recommendations

THE MEANS OF PROTECTING INDIVIDUAL PRIVACY
IN EVALUATION RESEARCH   8

    Physical Protection
    Legal Protection

CONCLUSION   15

APPENDIX A. CONFIDENTIALITY-PRESERVING MODES OF ACCESS TO FILES
             AND TO INTERFILE EXCHANGE FOR USEFUL STATISTICAL
             ANALYSIS

             By Donald T. Campbell, Robert F. Boruch, Richard D.
             Schwartz, and Joseph Steinberg

APPENDIX B. A RESEARCHER'S SHIELD STATUTE: GUARDING AGAINST
             THE COMPULSORY DISCLOSURE OF RESEARCH DATA

             By Paul Nejelski and Howard Peyser

SUMMARY AND RECOMMENDATIONS

The Committee on Federal Agency Evaluation Research is releasing this report in hopes that it will arouse informed debate on an important public issue: how to protect the privacy of individuals who provide information about themselves to be used in the evaluation of federal government programs.[1]

The issue is difficult because it involves reconciling two important objectives: government accountability and individual privacy. Holding the government accountable for its use of the taxpayers' money (and making informed decisions about future use of such money) necessitates evaluating the effectiveness of government programs in meeting the needs of the people they are supposed to serve. Such evaluation may require the collection of sensitive information from individuals as to how their health, employment, income, or other aspects of their lives have been altered by the government's efforts. The collection of such information entails risks to the individual's privacy--risks that the information collected for evaluation will be used for some other purpose to the detriment of the person who provided it.

The Committee believes that both objectives are important and that neither should be sacrificed to the other. Ways can and must be found to evaluate government programs without endangering the privacy of people who cooperate in such evaluation by providing information about themselves. To this end the Committee recommends:

(1) that all federal agencies engaging in evaluation research adopt rigorous procedures to ensure that data collected about individuals in the course of such research are kept strictly confidential and are not used for purposes other than such research or released in any way that permits identification of individuals;

---

[1] Throughout the body of this Report, the words "data" and "information" are used interchangeably and refer to facts or opinions that people give about themselves through written or oral responses to researchers. This meaning and usage also applies to Appendix A. In Appendix B (and in the Report's reference to that Appendix), the words "data" and "information" are also used interchangeably, but more broadly: they include not only the responses from research subjects but also researchers' work products, i.e., all materials resulting from all aspects of the research process.

(2) that consideration be given to enactment of a federal statute that would protect from subpoena information collected from individuals in the course of federal evaluation research and thus prevent such information from being used in law enforcement or other legal proceedings.

These recommendations and the reasoning behind them are discussed below.

THE NEED FOR PROTECTING INDIVIDUAL
PRIVACY IN EVALUATION RESEARCH

BACKGROUND OF THE COMMITTEE ON FEDERAL AGENCY EVALUATION RESEARCH

The Committee on Federal Agency Evaluation Research (COFAER) was set up in 1971 by the National Academy of Sciences at the request of (and with funding from) the U.S. Office of Economic Opportunity (OEO). The Committee was given a broad mandate to examine the government's activities in evaluation research and social policy experimentation and to recommend ways of making these activities more effective and useful. In particular, it was asked to examine the problem of confidentiality of data collected in the course of evaluation research and social experimentation and to recommend ways of protecting the privacy of individuals who provide such information to researchers.

The concern of the Office of Economic Opportunity with these issues arose both from a specific incident and from its general role as the spearhead of the government's "war on poverty." The Office of Economic Opportunity had been created as an experimental agency that would try out new programs, which if successful, might be transferred to more permanent agencies. Identification of such successful programs clearly necessitated substantial efforts to evaluate OEO-sponsored activities and, therefore, substantial interest in the problems of program evaluation.

The particular incident that precipitated OEO's acute concern with confidentiality occurred during the New Jersey income maintenance project--a major social experiment designed to measure the impact of various negative income tax plans on labor force behavior and other activities of low-income families.[2] Participants in the experiment were asked to complete detailed questionnaires about their income, employment, and other activities and were promised by the researchers that this information would be kept absolutely confidential. However, local law enforcement officers saw in the experiment an opportunity to check on welfare cheating and endeavored to get hold of the confidential information. The researchers in charge of the experiment found themselves in a

---

[2] See David N. Kershaw and Joseph C. Small, "Data Confidentiality and Privacy: Lessons from the New Jersey Negative Income Tax Experiment," Public Policy, 20:257-280 (Spring 1972).

difficult position. They had promised confidentiality to respondents in good faith, but it was by no means clear that they could honor that pledge if a court saw fit to issue a subpoena.

Distressed by the dilemmas of this incident, OEO officials asked the Committee to give special attention to the problem of confidentiality and to make recommendations for ways of ensuring confidentiality of data collected in future evaluations and experiments.

THE NEED FOR EVALUATION

The Office of Economic Opportunity was only the most conspicuous of the many federal agencies that were involved in the enormous expansion of social welfare programs in the 1960's, programs that provide cash, in-kind benefits, or human services directly to individuals and families. These programs--including Social Security, public assistance, Medicare and Medicaid, Head Start, manpower training, housing, and urban renewal--grew from about $23 billion or one-quarter of the federal budget in Fiscal Year 1960 to about $150 billion or roughly one-half of the federal budget in Fiscal Year 1975. And in such areas as drug abuse control and the administration of criminal justice, federal involvement and concern has become far more pervasive than is suggested by the relatively small amounts of federal money involved.

If the public is to make an intelligent assessment of how well the federal government is doing its job, it needs information on how federal programs are operating: who is being reached; how effective the programs are; at what cost results are being produced. It is also essential for the public and the Congress to have estimates of the costs and effects of alternative future programs before making decisions on the adoption of those programs, and sometimes the best way of estimating how a new policy would work is to carry out a small-scale experiment.

Evaluation research and social experimentation are extremely difficult. It is hard to identify precisely the objectives of government programs or to find valid measures of their effects. It is also difficult to design and execute experiments that accurately represent what would happen if a new program were actually adopted. Despite the difficulties, however, major efforts should be made to improve both the quantity and the quality of evaluation results available to decision makers. Indeed, for government officials, legislators, and the public to make decisions about national programs without careful consideration of the costs and probable effects of present and future policies would be both inefficient and irresponsible.

Accountability to the public requires not only that evaluations of public programs be carried out, but that they be available for public scrutiny. Furthermore, government officials should be given the sole responsibility for evaluating their own programs. Therefore, it is essential that government officials or agencies other than the program sponsor and researchers in the private sector engage in independent evaluations and that they have access to experimentation and evaluation data collected by the program sponsors (whether government agencies or contractors) so that they can reanalyze and reinterpret them.

PROTECTION OF PRIVACY

The need for these data runs into conflict with the deeply held American value of personal privacy. Louis D. Brandeis called the right to be let alone "the right most valued by civilized men."[3] The framers of the Bill of Rights took great pains to guard private citizens against arbitrary and unreasonable intrusions of government into their personal affairs. In recent years, however, new technologies--such as wiretapping, electronic surveillance, and computers--have posed threats to individual privacy undreamed of by the authors of the Constitution and have challenged the legal and political system to devise new rules and procedures to protect that privacy. The large-scale collection of information about individuals for the purpose of experimenting with and evaluating government programs also poses a threat to individual privacy.

The problem is complicated by the fact that the most important questions about the effectiveness of human service programs relate to their effects over a fairly long period of time. Evaluating such programs requires following the same people to see what happened to them--how their training affected their income or how their treatment in prison affected their criminal record. It may also require obtaining a great many different pieces of information together on one person, perhaps from different sources, so that the effects of a program can be sorted out from the effects of other influences on that person's life. Thus, evaluating transfers and services to people may involve building dossiers on individuals and using them for a long time.

Federal programs affecting people are likely to grow both absolutely and relatively in the future. Hence, informed decision making about federal activities will require more and more evaluations based on sensitive information about individual behavior. Improved survey design and management, including improved statistical sampling procedures, questionnaire design, analytic techniques, and data processing capabilities make such evaluation feasible, but the increased collection of data from and about individuals increases the threat to privacy and the danger that these data will be misused. A desire for openess and accountability in government further compounds the problem. The use of outside evaluators and the reanalysis of data by outside analysts increase the danger that individual information will fall into the wrong hands and be used for purposes other than evaluation.

It is necessary to devise workable procedures for facilitating evaluation and accountability while continuing to protect individual privacy. The competing goals must be continually balanced: it is not in the national interest to sacrifice privacy for the sake of evaluation and accountability, nor would it be desirable to write such strict procedures to safeguard individual privacy that it becomes impossible to evaluate or reevaluate public programs or to gain insights into the potential costs and effects of new policies.

Ultimately, effective protection of individual privacy is a sine qua non of usable evaluation and experimentation. People simply will not cooperate in giving accurate information about themselves to researchers and evaluators unless they are assured that the information will not be used against them by bill collectors, tax collectors, or neighborhood gossips. Hence, some means of

---

[3] Dissent in Olmstead v. U.S., 277 U.S. 438, 48 S.Ct. 564 (1928).

assuring that information will be kept confidential is essential, not only to protect individual privacy as an end in itself, but also to make possible valid experimentations and evaluations of public programs.

FINDINGS AND RECOMMENDATIONS

The Committee does not believe it is possible, at this time, to formulate definitive procedures that will ensure both protection of individual privacy and adequate data for experimentation and evaluation. The Committee's mandate, though broad, covered only federal activities, and the Committee has concluded that a definitive review of the problem must take into account the full range of research activities. The Committee also believes that a much broader public debate on the competing values of individual privacy and government accountability by means of evaluation and experimentation is needed. Therefore, the Committee decided that its most useful contribution to this complex problem would be to present some specific proposals that can be the basis for wide discussion by those concerned with the problem both inside and outside the federal government.

The specific proposals included in this report cover two broad areas, corresponding to two distinct risks to the privacy of individuals who provide information about themselves to evaluators of social programs. One might be called the risk of <u>unauthorized misuse</u> of sensitive data. This is the risk that identifiable information on people collected for purposes of evaluation will fall into the hands of unauthorized persons who want to use it against an individual--blackmailers, sales people, bill collectors, etc. The danger is that such persons might get hold of the actual records showing individual names and addresses as well as private information or that they might be able to identify an individual even without the name and address from the information itself, perhaps by matching information with public records. The problem here is one of <u>physical protection</u> of the data--devising ways of reducing the number of people with access to identifiable records and of reducing the probability that individuals can be identified even after names and addresses or other identifiers, such as Social Security numbers, have been removed.

The other risk might be described as that of <u>official misuse</u> for law enforcement or other official purposes of data originally obtained from people for evaluation purposes. Here the problem is how to provide <u>legal protection</u> so that people who cooperate with an evaluation by providing information about their behavior can be assured that the information they provide will not be used for any other purpose, including law enforcement.

Early discussions convinced the Committee of the need for new procedures for the physical protection of confidential data, especially when data files are to be made available by the collecting agency for reanalysis by outside researchers and when evaluation requires the combination of information on the same people from more than one source. Therefore, the Committee asked Donald T. Campbell, Richard D. Schwartz, Robert F. Boruch, and Joseph Steinberg to consider this range of problems and make recommendations. Their paper, entitled "Confidentiality-Preserving Modes of Access to Files and to Interfile Exchange for Useful Statistical Analysis," is reproduced as Appendix A to this Report. The Committee deems it a valuable and major contribution to the debate and hopes it will be widely read and discussed by those concerned with the problem.

The Committee was also convinced by its consultation with experts in the field that legal protection of confidential information collected in the course of evaluation is required, but that difficult and controversial decisions would have to be made before the specific form of that protection could be formulated. One suggested form of legal protection is a "shield statute" for researchers, and the Committee invited one of its members, Paul Nejelski, and his colleague, Howard Peyser, to draft a statute and to submit a paper discussing the major issues that had to be resolved in drafting the statute and the reasons they favored the particular resolutions reflected in their proposed statute. Their paper, entitled "A Researcher's Shield Statute: Guarding Against the Compulsory Disclosure of Research Data," is reproduced as Appendix B to this Report. The Committee believes they have made a major contribution and that their statute is worthy of strong consideration and debate.

Based on its review of these papers and its own deliberation, the Committee recommends:

(1) that all federal agencies engaging in evaluation research adopt rigorous procedures to ensure that data collected about individuals in the course of such research are kept strictly confidential and are not used for purposes other than such research or released in any way that permits identification of individuals;

(2) that consideration be given to enactment of a federal statute that would protect from subpoena information collected from individuals in the course of federal evaluation research and thus prevent such information from being used in law enforcement or other legal proceedings.

The remainder of this Report serves as an introduction to the appended papers and summarizes the Committee's views about physical and legal protection of confidential information in social experimentation and evaluation research. Because of the origin and chief concern of the Committee, the Report deals mainly with federally funded evaluation research, but the problems discussed arise in connection with other types of research on human behavior and the Committee believes that any solutions offered should be applicable to all such research. It should also be noted that the Committee focused only on the privacy of individuals; the more complex problem of the privacy of groups or institutions (e.g., schools, unions) was not studied.

THE MEANS OF PROTECTING INDIVIDUAL PRIVACY IN EVALUATION RESEARCH

PHYSICAL PROTECTION

A pledge to hold information confidential is a means of striking a balance between an individual's right to privacy and the public's need to evaluate the effects of government programs or experiments. An evaluator asks people sensitive questions about their behavior, but promises to use the information exclusively for the purpose of evaluating the program or experiment and not to release it in a form that would permit identification of the individuals who furnished the information.

Researchers and evaluators clearly have two strong incentives to honor the confidentiality pledge. Their personal integrity--or the reputation of their research organization--is at stake, and their ability to obtain additional data from people in the current or future evaluation research projects will be jeopardized if the pledge of confidentiality is broken. There are two major risks to the researchers' ability to keep the confidentiality promise: (1) that someone will get hold of the records containing identified individual information and use the information to injure the person who gave it or for the private benefit of someone else; (2) that even after a person's name and address have been removed from the record, someone will be able to identify that person from the pieces of information given and use the information to that person's detriment.

The first danger--that identified records will be stolen or misused--clearly increases with the number of people who have access to these records and with the extent to which these people lack a continuing commitment to evaluation research. If evaluations could be carried out by a single qualified researcher who conducted his or her own interviews, made a promise of confidentiality, and personally wrote up the results, the risk would be small. But modern evaluation research often involves a large quantity of data and a large number of people processing that data--interviewers, coders, key punch operators, computer programmers, and computer operators--in addition to statisticians and other researchers. Hence, the risk of misuse is significant, and rules for handling information need to be carefully formulated and strictly enforced.

The Committee feels strongly that every agency sponsoring evaluation research should have clear guidelines designed to minimize the risk of mishandling sensitive personal information. These guidelines should be strictly followed by its own evaluators and by grantees and contractors involved in evaluation research, and severe penalties should be imposed on violators.

The following rules should govern such guidelines:

(1) Sensitive information should not be collected unless it is clearly necessary to the evaluation and is to be used.

Social scientists have a tendency to load additional questions onto survey instruments because "it would be interesting to know that." Such loading should be severely discouraged, especially if the information is sensitive and might damage the respondent if revealed.

(2) Where it is feasible and does not undermine the validity of the evaluation, the anonymity of the respondent should be preserved from the beginning by not collecting identifying information at all.

Unfortunately, the collection of anonymous information usually limits the usefulness and validity of the evaluation. If identifying information is not collected, the data provided by the respondent cannot be checked. In particular, there is no way to follow up those who fail to give complete information or to estimate the likely error introduced by such incomplete responses. When the evaluation requires information from the same people at successive times (longitudinal data), identifiers must be collected so that the researchers can return for the later information. In many evaluations, the real interest centers on change brought about by a government program, and it is necessary to interview individuals more than once in order to estimate this change. Nevertheless, where highly sensitive information is needed--for example, when the behavior of interest is clearly criminal--the only way to collect such information without risk to the respondent may be to preserve absolute anonymity from the beginning.

(3) Identifying information, such as name and address or Social Security number, should be removed from the individual records at the earliest possible stage of analysis and replaced by a code number. The key linking this code number to the identifying information should be stored in a safe place and access to it severely limited. This key should be destroyed as soon as it is no longer needed.

The objectives of these procedures should be to reduce to an absolute minimum the number of people who have access to identified records and to make sure that these people are fully committed to honoring the pledge of confidentiality and subject to severe penalties if they do not.

There have been relatively few problems of protecting identified information when evaluations have been carried out by federal employees and the data processed within a federal agency. Usually, however, evaluation research is carried out by private researchers or research organizations under contract with the government, and data are processed by non-government computer installations. In such situations, the contract should specify strict procedures for safeguarding identified confidential data. Interviewers and other employees handling identified data should have to sign a pledge not to reveal the information and should be subject to specified penalties if they break the pledge. Security arrangements should be specified, and the government should make sure they are observed and impose penalties if they are not. Special attention must be paid to safeguarding identified records that are stored in computers, especially computers that are accessible to many users on a time-sharing basis.

The safeguards needed become more complicated when additional researchers (other than the person or organization that originally collected and analyzed the data) want access for reanalysis. Such reanalysis is useful not only to get an independent check on the original evaluation, but also to use data collected for evaluation purposes to test additional hypotheses about human behavior. The information collected from families in the course of the New Jersey income maintenance experiment, for example, is not only useful in evaluating the particular income maintenance plans tried out in that experiment, but also provides a rich source of data on low income families that can be used to explore a variety of hypotheses about labor force participation, spending patterns, and other family economic behavior.

It is essential, however, that reanalysis be carried out in ways that will not jeopardize the privacy of the respondents. Two basic procedures are possible. One is to release data files to outside researchers only after all identifiers have been removed and after ensuring that individuals cannot be identified from the information given about them.[4] The other is not to release any raw data at all, but to provide funding so that the original researcher can respond to the requests of outside researchers and provide reanalysis to their specifications.

Under some circumstances it is useful to merge data on people from two or more confidential sources in order to improve the validity of evaluation research. For example, in comparing the effectiveness of two educational curricula for children from different socio-economic levels, children's test scores and other school performance data would be available from one source while information on their family background would be obtained from another. Merging two sets of data might be indispensible to an evaluation, but care should be taken that the merging process does not jeopardize respondents' privacy. The key necessary to match two sets of data should be accessible to as few people as possible and should be returned to safekeeping or destroyed as soon as possible. Care should be taken to ensure that the new merged data set is not released in raw form if there is any significant chance that individuals can be identified from the data even after name, address, or other obvious identifiers have been removed. Methods of protecting privacy when more than one data file is utilized are discussed in detail in Appendix A.

Even after name, address, Social Security number, and other positive identifiers have been removed from individual records, there remains a risk that a malevolent and persistent person could take the information given in an unidentified record and track down the subject person or family. The potential for this kind of detective work rises as the number of pieces of information given about each individual or family increases; hence, merging two or more data files increases the risk of identification. It is especially high when a person can be identified as a member of a small group--for example, residents of a particular census tract or pediatricians in Nevada. Risk of identification is also increased when a piece of information in the confidential file is also a matter of public record, such as birth, marriage, or death records or property taxes and deeds.

Hence, if confidential data are to be released for reanalysis by additional researchers, extreme care must be taken to frustrate those who might try to match the records to real individuals. Variables that identify the person as

---

[4]This point is discussed further below.

a resident of a small area or member of a small group should be removed from the record, along with variables that might be matched with public records. Another technique for impeding the identification of individuals is error innoculation, which involves actually altering the information on an individual record in a way that will not invalidate statistical analysis, but will leave anyone with access to the record unsure whether it is a real or a doctored record.[5]

LEGAL PROTECTION

The last several years have seen the emergence of a new threat to the confidentiality of data collected from people in the course of evaluation research: that a researcher will be legally compelled to reveal such information to a court or to Congress. Several incidents have brought the threat forcibly to the attention of the research community.

In the New Jersey negative income tax experiment mentioned above, the researchers felt strongly that protecting the privacy of participants in the experiment was not only right, but essential to the success of the experiment. To evaluate the effects of a negative income tax, they needed accurate information on individuals' earnings, hours worked, expenditures, living arrangements, etc. People would be reluctant to participate or to give honest answers if they thought the information might be made public or used against them. Moreover, public identification of the participants would subject them to publicity and possible pressure that might change their behavior and invalidate the results of the experiment. Hence, both OEO and Mathematica (the organization carrying out the experiment) made assiduous efforts to assure respondents that the information they gave would be held strictly confidential and used only to evaluate the experiment. Interviewers and other employees were required to sign a "confidentiality agreement" and strict rules were laid down within the project for preventing the release of identified information.

To the surprise and dismay of the experimenters, however, threats to the privacy of respondents arose from two directions. First, the Mercer County, New Jersey prosecutor, seeing an opportunity to use experimental information to find out if any families in the experiment were collecting illegal welfare payments, subpoenaed the records. The experimenters negotiated with the prosecutor, offering to reimburse the government for any illegal overpayments rather than subject the respondents to prosecution and publicity, but in the end believed there were no valid legal grounds for resisting the subpoenas.

At the same time, the Senate Finance Committee, which was debating welfare reform, became interested in the experiment and asked for identified individual family records. The experimenters eventually convinced the Committee it did not need identified case histories, but realized that if a showdown had come there would not have been any legal grounds for resisting a Congressional subpoena.

This and other incidents demonstrate that researchers can no longer in good conscience promise that information collected for evaluation purposes will

---

[5]This technique is discussed further in Appendix A.

be kept confidential unless they have a specific legal basis for the promise. If they are being honest with their respondents, they must alert them to the danger that the information they give might be made available to the courts or to the Congress. Such warnings are likely to decrease both the proportion of people willing to give information needed for evaluation research and the honesty of the responses.

Resolution of this dilemma involves a balancing of values. There is a strong public interest in enforcing the laws and making evidence available to courts, but these interests may conflict with other values, such as protecting the privacy of the individual from government snooping or arbitrary search and seizure of personal property. Deference to these other values has led to Constitutional and other limitations on the admissibility of certain kinds of evidence, such as that obtained by illegal wiretapping. In these instances society is willing to take the risk that some criminal acts will be unpunished in order to guard against greater threats to the welfare of all citizens.

Similar reasoning has led to the exclusion of certain "privileged" communications, such as those between lawyer and client, from consideration as evidence in a court proceeding. The general reasoning is that society has an interest in fostering certain exchanges of information that would be jeopardized if their confidential nature could not be guaranteed, and that this interest outweighs the interest of producing additional evidence. The interest in encouraging people with legal problems to seek the advice of lawyers and to speak freely to them is deemed considerable and depends on the assurance that the lawyers will not be required to testify against their clients in court. Similarly, confidences between husband and wife, priest and penitent, and doctor and patient have been absolutely or partly protected by common law or statutory privileges. The Committee believes that society must now consider whether the public interest would be served by making the information furnished in the course of evaluation research or social experimentation a class of privileged communication.

Arguments against an extension of some form of privilege to communications between researcher and respondent range from the practical problems of defining *bona fide* research (or researchers) and possible impediments to prosecution of illegal activities to broader considerations such as the current trend in society toward openness and tendencies of many legal experts to resist expanding the class of privileged communication. The Committee has no desire to protect illegal activities or weaken the effectiveness of the courts or of the Congressional power of inquiry, but it believes that the benefits of fostering a free and honest flow of information from individuals to evaluators of public programs is worth the decrease in otherwise available data.

It should be noted that this privilege would not deprive the courts or Congress of any substantial evidentiary resource currently available. Evaluation research and social experimentation are relatively new activities that neither the courts nor the Congress have previously relied on for any significant amount of evidence. Nor, in the long run, would the privilege deprive the courts or the Congress of evidence that would have been available lacking the privilege; if researchers cannot guarantee the confidentiality of information from respondents, much experimentation and evaluation will not be undertaken and the data will be available to no one.

On balance, therefore, the Committee concluded that, in the public interest, serious consideration should be given to protecting the confidentiality of information given by respondents for the purpose of bona fide evaluation research.

The Committee then turned to the difficult questions of how the privilege should be created and how broad or narrow it should be. Is a statute needed? If so, what kind of communications should be protected, under what circumstances, and with what exceptions?

It has been argued that no statute is needed because the Constitutional guarantee of freedom of the press, which protects journalists from having to disclose their sources in court, by extension protects researchers from being compelled to disclose information gathered for research purposes, since one product of research is publication of the results. Without this extension, the basis for statutory protection of researchers would be very different from that for journalists, since protection of news sources derives from an explicit Constitutional guarantee and protection of research sources from only an implicit right of privacy. Even if extension of the Constitutional guarantee were to be accepted, however, it might afford little protection since recent court decisions have gone against journalists who have refused to disclose their sources in court. For this reason, consideration is currently being given to the enactment of a federal "shield statute," although there is no unanimity in the news or legal profession as to the advantages or scope of such a statute.

The Committee believes that very serious consideration should be given to a researcher's shield statute and that the most valuable contribution the Committee could make to an informed debate would be to ask legal experts to draft such a statute and to publish it to stimulate discussion. The Nejelski and Peyser paper, Appendix B, is the result of that request, and the Committee hopes that it will be widely discussed and debated by lawyers, researchers, legislators, and the interested public.

In brief, the draft statute would create a new class of privileged communication--communication between the subject of research and the researcher--analogous to privileged communications between client and lawyer or patient and doctor. If the statute were in force, a researcher could not be compelled by a subpoena issued by a court or a legislative committee to testify about research subjects or to produce information gathered in the course of research.

The researcher's shield statute proposed by Nejelski and Peyser reflects a position that might be described as "maximum protection" for research and researchers very broadly defined. It covers not only evaluation research, but all research in the public interest; it protects not only information communicated by individuals to the researcher but the researcher's observations and intermediate work product, such as unfinished manuscripts; and it is an absolute privilege, applying under all conditions unless waived by both the subject and the researcher. The Committee believes that this "maximum protection" position deserves serious consideration; however, some members of the Committee would favor a statute that is narrower in one or more respects than that proposed by Nejelski and Peyser.

Three kinds of limitations to "maximum protection" were considered by the Committee:

(1) Limiting the privilege to federal agency evaluation research.

The original concern of the Committee was with "federal agency evaluation research," meaning research carried out by or under the sponsorship of a federal government agency and designed to estimate the effectiveness of a federal program, project, demonstration, or experiment. The Committee feels that the public importance of such research is clearly demonstrable and that the usefulness of the research results is clearly jeopardized when confidentiality cannot be guaranteed.

It would be possible to draft a federal statute creating a research privilege that applied only to federal agency evaluation research and some members of the Committee would favor this course of action. Proponents of this position believe that it is far easier to demonstrate to legislators the public usefulness of federal evaluation research than of research in general. They also fear that too broad a definition might invite abuse of the privilege by persons with tenuous connections to genuine research. Nejelski and Peyser, however, rejected this narrow approach because they saw no valid reason why evaluation sponsored by federal agencies should be singled out for protection and no useful way to distinguish evaluation research from other research. It is society's broader interest in the knowledge created by research that Nejelski and Peyser believe should be protected by the creation of a research privilege. They would specify only that the research must be in the "public interest," and not, for example, market research for the benefit of a private company.

(2) Limiting the communications and materials protected.
All members of the Committee see a clear interest in protecting identifiable information communicated by an individual to a researcher. Such information would normally be in the form of questionnaires, notes, or other records of interviews. Nejelski and Peyser would go further and protect all of a researcher's records and "work product," whether containing identifiable information or not. Some members of the Committee believe that extending the privilege to all of a researcher's work product is unnecessary and might invite suppression of evaluation results that are unfavorable to the sponsoring agency.

(3) Narrowing the scope of the privilege.
In general, privileges can be waived by the party whose privacy is being protected (the lawyer's client or the doctor's patient) and do not apply under certain circumstances (e.g., a client's communication to his lawyer concerning future crimes). Nejelski and Peyser propose the creation of a more comprehensive privilege, which could be waived only by both researcher and subject and which would cover all communications, including discussion of future crime. Some members of the Committee feel this position gives too heavy a weight to the value of protecting research.

These and related issues can and should be debated, but the Committee feels strongly that some kind of legal protection of research must be considered, to guarantee that respondents who give information about themselves to researchers--especially researchers evaluating the effectiveness of federal programs--need not fear that the information will be revealed to their detriment in a court or to an investigative body. Without such protection, it will become more and more difficult to obtain the information needed for valid evaluation of the effects of government programs.

CONCLUSION

The Committee believes that evaluation of government programs is very much in the public interest and should not endanger the privacy of individuals who give information about themselves. It will not be easy to work out procedures and legal arrangements that balance the conflicting objectives of fostering accountability in government and protecting individual privacy. Special efforts must be made in two areas: (1) protecting evaluation research data from accidental release or malicious misuse by unauthorized persons; (2) protecting people who give information about themselves in the course of evaluation research or social experimentation from having that information used in a court or legislative inquiry. The Committee believes that these efforts should receive high-priority attention in federal agencies, the Congress, and the research community. It is the Committee's hope that this Report and its appendices will contribute to informed debate on these issues.

APPENDIX A

CONFIDENTIALITY-PRESERVING MODES OF ACCESS TO FILES AND TO

INTERFILE EXCHANGE FOR USEFUL STATISTICAL ANALYSIS

Donald T. Campbell, Robert F. Boruch,

Richard D. Schwartz, and Joseph Steinberg*

*The authors are indebted to Professor Tore Dalenius for a careful review of an earlier draft of this manuscript. The efforts of Donald T. Campbell and Robert F. Boruch have been supported in part by grants from the Russell Sage Foundation, by National Science Foundation Grant GSOC-7103704, and by National Institute of Education Grant NIE-C-74-0115. Portions of an earlier draft of this report have been used by Boruch and Campbell as a basis for pages 261-269 of H. W. Riecken, R. F. Boruch, D. T. Campbell, T. K. Glennan, J Pratt, A. Rees, and W. Williams, Social experimentation: A method for planning and evaluating social intervention, New York: Academic Press, 1974. The resulting duplication is retained with the permission of Academic Press. The effort by Joseph Steinberg is in his private capacity; no official support or endorsement is intended nor should be inferred.

CONFIDENTIALITY-PRESERVING MODES OF ACCESS TO FILES AND TO INTERFILE EXCHANGE FOR USEFUL STATISTICAL ANALYSIS

INTRODUCTORY OVERVIEW

Some examples: (1) Achievement test scores and parental interviews from a Head Start evaluation project are subjected to statistical reanalyses by other scientists, who correct and extend the original findings. (2) The Bureau of the Census releases a one percent sample of interview data for sociologists and geographers to use in scientific studies. (3) The success of graduates of a job training program is ascertained by using Social Security Administration records on their later earnings and unemployment insurance payments.

These exemplify important uses of data archives, potentially of great value in improving our ability to solve social problems and to evaluate the usefulness of ameliorative programs. Such research utilizations of data files should be greatly increased if we are to optimally evaluate new social programs in the future. At the same time, if improperly done, such uses could violate the promises of confidentiality and increase the individual's risk of blackmail, invidious gossip, or arrest. This is the problem discussed in this paper.

At present, there is great concern about invasion of privacy and confidentiality and about the threat to individual freedom represented by data banks. Such concerns are currently much stronger than are demands for increased objectivity in the evaluation of governmental programs. It is our belief, detailed in this paper, that both concerns can be reconciled--that data archive use for program evaluation can be achieved without increasing the dangers of invasion of privacy. But we also believe that the means of such reconciliation are too little recognized and that there is a real danger of ill-considered solutions to the privacy problem that would needlessly preclude the use of archives in program evaluation. At its worst, the privacy issue becomes a rationalization for evading meaningful program evaluation.

The present analysis starts out by assuming the existence of administrative records and of archived statistical research data and then asks how both of these can be further used to generate non-individual statistical products without increasing the risks to individuals that are already implicit in these existing files.[1] Such a focus is tangential to many of the main concerns in the discussion of the threats of data banks. While we favor a number of the current proposals for the reform of government data archiving, both present practice and these reforms are compatible with the recommendations in this paper.

Thus, although not the focus of this paper, we join others in a number of recommendations on the management of data archives:

1. Administrative data collectors and evaluation researchers should refrain from collecting sensitive personal data not directly relevant to the government's legitimate concerns appropriate to the transaction at hand.

2. Identifying information should not be collected at all; that is, respondents should be kept anonymous from the beginning where this is compatible with the purposes of the evaluation.

3. For the purposes here represented, there would be no loss and perhaps some gain if individuals were given a copy of their own data at the time it is filed, with the opportunity to correct it if necessary and with the right to future access. (Much of this is already achieved for Social Security Administration and Internal Revenue Service files.)

4. In regard to the desirability of restricting the uses of data to those which the individual anticipated and was agreeable to when providing the data, it would probably be desirable if the forms used for data collection (e.g., income tax returns) announced that the data would also be used for statistical summaries in which the individual would be _unidentifiable_.

5. Restrictions would be desirable to prevent any secondary use of archived data for "intelligence" or investigatory purposes, that is, for actions or descriptions targeted on the individual; all secondary uses of data would be restricted to statistical products in which individuals were unidentifiable.

6. For statistical research data files, individual identifiers should be replaced with code numbers for data processing

---

[1]"Statistical" has unfortunately acquired two meanings in recent privacy discussions, both of which we want to represent here. The Privacy Act of 1974 (Public Law 93-579 8552a(a)(6)) uses "statistical" to designate data collected originally for research rather than administrative purposes: "the term 'statistical record' means a record in a system of records maintained for statistical research or reporting purposes only and not used in whole or in part in making any determination about an identifiable individual . . ."

In the second usage, "statistical" designates averages, percentages, standard deviations, correlation coefficients, etc., created from the individual data existing in either administrative files or research-generated records. Since these statistical products summarize individual data from many persons, their publication can usually be done in ways protecting individual privacy, by means discussed in this paper.

and computer storage, and the code key kept under tight security. For administrative data files, this may not always be feasible, but certainly should be required for any computer memory storage on a time-sharing basis.

7. Formal rules and guidelines should be promulgated to guarantee high standards of confidentiality and security management on the part of all data file staff.

8. For the data uses we advocate, a unified national data bank is not required. Such a data bank is feared because it multiplies the power of a corrupt employee to blackmail or of the government to police the individuals on whom data are recorded.

On the other hand, there are some recommended reforms of public record-keeping that would preclude the uses here advocated and that we regard as both needless and contrary to the public interest:

1. Abolition of the use of Social Security numbers for all but Social Security Administration files. Our recommendation is quite the opposite, namely, that Social Security numbers be recorded where possible. The abolition recommendation was designed to preclude merging files into larger data banks. Through the "mutually insulated file linkage" described in this paper, some types of file linkage can be achieved <u>without</u> merging, i.e., in a manner that prevents either file from acquiring identifiable individual information from the other file.[2] This procedure does require, however, that common identifiers, such as names and Social Security numbers, exist in each file. We believe that were this procedure adopted, the reasons for the suggested prohibition on Social Security numbers would be eliminated.

2. The destruction of personal data files after a specified period, say five or ten years. Many social innovations call for longer-term statistical follow-ups that would be precluded by such a rule.

3. The requirement of a specific, separate permission statement and explicit informed consent for each separate statistical <u>research</u> use of an administrative file. We regard this recommendation as contrary to the public interest as well as needless when no indivdually identifiable data are being released from the file, as in procedures described below.

4. Elimination of all individually identified files in any form. Needless to say, we regard this as impossible for administrative files in their administrative use, unneeded for protection of individuals since this can adequately be done in other ways,

---

[2]"Merging files," means the complete combining of files so that all of the individual data from one file gets transferred into the other or into a new combined file in an individually identifiable manner. "File linkage" is the more inclusive term, covering not only file merging (the most complete form of linkage), but also other ways of relating the information in one file to the information in another. In the second part of this paper we discuss four modes of file linkage, short of merging, aimed at preserving privacy of individual records.

and seriously detrimental to our capacity for program evaluation.

The requirements for safeguarding confidentiality are, of course, the responsibility of the administrators of each specific data file. The precautions and procedures necessary will vary from setting to setting. This paper focuses on the most cautious and conservative approaches, not to recommend that they be required in all settings, but rather to emphasize that, for even the most sensitive settings, there are safe modes of access that will permit important statistical analyses. These conservative approaches do set limits to the degree of refinement possible in the statistical analyses, and, to avoid such costs, one should not use a more conservative approach than is called for by the requirements of the situation.

The major sections of this paper discuss specific procedures under two main headings. The first is designated <u>intrafile analysis by outsiders</u>. In this category, all of the statistical analyses under consideration are to be done within a single data file. This category is exemplified by the U.S. Census Bureau's Decennial Census public use one percent and 0.1 percent samples which are released for social science research purposes, or by the Social Security Administration's one percent Continuous Work History Sample (CWHS). In the experience of the Office of Economic Opportunity (OEO), such uses are encountered in the release of data for reanalysis from the evaluations of Head Start, Performance Contracting, and the New Jersey Negative Income Tax Experiment (NJNITE).[3] Six classes of procedures are considered for intrafile analysis by outsiders, concluding with the following recommendations:

Deletion of known identifiers (name, Social Security number) is insufficient unless also accompanied by restrictions in number and refinement of data on variables that are publicly available elsewhere, or unless accompanied by error inoculation on public variables, especially by additive normal error;

Microaggregated release is acceptable, albeit statistically costly;

Best of all is in-file capacity as a public utility to run outsiders' statistical analyses, accompanied by randomized rounding of frequency tabulations to prevent disclosure through comparisons of sets of results.

The secondary category of utilization considered is <u>interfile exchange of confidential data</u>, where one or both files are confidential and the objective is to relate variables across files in statistical analyses. (Most conservatively, such exchanges can be done without merging files, i.e., with neither file acquiring the other's confidential data.) Examples of this occur when Social Security Administration data are used to evaluate Job Corps training

---

[3]The official title of this project, as evidenced by its final report, is the New Jersey Graduated Work Incentive Experiment (Watts and Rees, 1973). See also the special issue of <u>The Journal of Human Resources</u>, Spring, 1974. However, since it is much better known as the New Jersey Negative Income Tax Experiment, and since a number of publications will continue to use that name (e.g., Kershaw, 1972; 1974), it has seemed most convenient to retain that title. Because of the origins of COFAER and the original requests to it, the NJNITE is a major source of illustrations, hypothetical for the most part, in what follows.

programs, when the Census Current Population Survey data are related to IRS Statistics of Income data derived from income tax reports, or, conjecturally, if NJNITE interview data were to be related to withholding tax information or to FICA earnings. For such purposes, this paper emphasizes the most conservative of several procedures: mutually insulated file linkage with random deletion of one respondent from each list. Link file brokerage, a widely discussed procedure, is considerably less conservative, but may be a useful strategy if adequate protection for confidentiality can be assured. There are also settings with confidentiality safeguards and legal protection from subpoena in which the still less conservative approach of direct file merging provides reasonable safeguards. Full merging has the advantage of preserving full statistical information on all relationships among all variables for any analysis or reanalysis. Where this approach is used, it would be very important for the merged file to have in-file capacity to run outsiders' statistical analyses (as discussed more extensively in the next section).

INTRAFILE ANALYSIS BY OUTSIDERS

Deletion of Identifiers

It is customary in releasing data for reanalysis to delete names, Social Security numbers, and addresses from the data on individuals. In some settings this may provide sufficient protection in that it may not increase the respondent's loss of privacy or increase the risks of breach of confidentiality. In other settings, deletion of identifiers is an insufficient safeguard. Two features seem crucial: the number of items of information on each person and the availability of those items on public lists with names attached. For example, deletion of identifiers might be sufficient for a 0.1 percent sample of the 1970 Census because of the extremely scattered nature of the sample and the absence of parallel lists. However, even in this case, if census tract, age, and specialty are given for a low-frequency, visibly listed profession, such as M.D., individual identification could frequently be made and the other information on the record thereby identified with a specific person, thus making it possible for a corrupt user to infringe upon the M.D.'s privacy (Hansen, 1971).

Where the research population is compact and where some of the variables are conveniently recorded with names on public or semi-public lists (here designated as <u>public variables</u>), the deletion of identifiers is less adequate. Thus, for a study conducted within a single school, even the date and place of birth are usually sufficient to reveal names. (Specific birth date in combination with birth place probably should always be treated as a personal identifier.)

In the case of the NJNITE, data tapes are now being released to outside users through the Data Center of The Institute for Research on Poverty of the University of Wisconsin. It was decided in this case that a thorough deletion of identifiers provided adequate protection. This deletion covered names, addresses, exact birth places and birth dates, Social Security numbers, and, in addition, the names of doctors, teachers, etc. These data have been deleted not only from the released tapes, but also from the original interviews preserved in microfilm.

Crude Report Categories for, and Restriction of, Public Variables

For public variables in the confidential file (variables that are readily available elsewhere with names attached), cruder report categories should be used in the data released, to the level needed to prevent disclosure: e.g., county rather than census tract, year of birth rather than day or month, profession but not specialty within profession, etc. For variables unique to the research project (unique variables), which therefore do not exist on other lists with names attached, this precaution is not necessary. Thus, for a multi-item attitude test or for an achievement test, individual item responses and exact total scores can be made available without jeopardizing confidentiality. (Such data probably should be made available because of their relevance to the estimation of error for use in generating alternate statistical adjustments, an issue of ever-increasing concern.)

Even with crude report categories on such public variables as geographic area, places and years of schooling, age, profession, etc., if there are enough such variables, combinations emerge in which only one or two persons occur and discovery of individual identity becomes possible. Thus, there should be a minimum lower bound restriction on the cell sizes of the full combination of public variables. For example, the rule might be adopted that there should be no combination of public variables yielding a frequency less than three persons. (Fellegi and Phillips, 1974; Hansen, 1971; Hoffman and Miller, 1970). Recoding of variables using still cruder report categories, or complete deletion of public variables, should be done until the chosen criterion is achieved. Before a criterion is chosen, tests of the anonymity-breaking potentials of various criteria should be tried out using actual bodies of data and publicly available lists.

These restrictions are obviously at the cost of some potential statistical analyses, particularly if some public variables have to be eliminated entirely. It might be thought that this could be avoided by releasing to each given user only some of the public variables, permitting the user to specify which public variables were of highest priority to the particular work. This strategy would suffice if there were only one user on one occasion or if users could be kept from sharing their data sets. But this seems impossible to guarantee, and such sharing would permit discovery of identity. For example, if user Alpha received public variables P_1 and P_2 plus all unique variables U_1 through U_n, while user Beta received public variables P_3 and P_4 plus all unique variables U_1 through U_n, they could easily employ the shared unique variables to achieve perfect matches and thus generate a complete, merged deck with P_1, P_2, P_3, and P_4 on each person. This full set of public variables might then be sufficient to identify individuals with the help of public lists.

Random Subsample Release

The last-mentioned problem of multiple users sharing differentially deleted data sets and thereby gaining increased ability to disclose individual identities can be greatly attenuated by providing each user with a different randomly selected subset of the data. This approach is obviously most usable for files containing a large number of individuals. It provides most protection where the sample is a small portion of the total available population and when the public and unique variables are few enough in number and crude enough in categories so that many persons end up with identical patterns and individual identification is precluded.

Microaggregation

Feige and Watts (Feige and Watts, 1970; Watts, 1972) have developed a technique of microaggregation for the release of census data on firms, as a substitute for the release of individual data. This approach has been recommended as a general approach to the release of confidential data. The idea of microaggregation is to create many synthetic average persons and to release the data on these rather than on individuals. Thus, instead of releasing individual data on the 1,200 participants of the NJNITE, as has been done, hypothetically one might group the data into 240 sets of five each and release average data on every variable for each set (probably with within-set variance as well as mean). Outside users could then do all of their secondary analyses on these 240 synthetic persons.

Feige, Watts, and their colleagues have done such analyses on Federal Reserve Board data on banks and have been able to compare microaggregate analyses with individual data analyses. Their conclusion is clear that such microaggregation is much more useful than no release of data at all. It results in a loss of statistical efficiency, but does not necessarily bias the statistical estimates. For most conceivable grouping variables, anonymity and confidentiality are preserved at the individual level.

The actual acceptable basis for microaggregation must be thought through in detail for every specific body of data. The following preliminary suggestions hypothetically illustrate the problem for the NJNITE. For most purposes, aggregation should probably keep intact the experimental design, that is, aggregation should be done within treatments and in comparability across treatments. (There would be many more such aggregates in the 640-person control group than in one of the experimental groups that average around 80 persons, but each one of the experimental group aggregates should be identifiable as parallel to certain control aggregates, etc.) In the Feige and Watts discussion, local region is a preferred basis of aggregation. In the NJNITE, cities differ considerably in time of initiation of the experiment and in attrition rates. Therefore, city should be used as a basis for aggregation, and possibly region within city. Ethnicity would be wanted for some uses, but with an initial sampling model assigning as few as 16 cases per experimental treatment per city, comparability would be hard to maintain for any variable not blocked on initially. (Aggregating by initial blocking seems a reasonable rule in most social experiments.) If complete data cases are aggregated separately from those lost through attrition, comparability is jeopardized because the attrition in the NJNITE is differential, being greatest in the control and low payment treatments. Possibly, attrition could be handled by reading out for each variable not only mean and variance but also the number of persons on which data were computed, basing the mean on those cases providing data.

The variables used as a basis for aggregation must be independent of sampling variation to assure that an estimator (of slope, say, in a linear function) based on aggregated data is unbiased. Since the dependent variable is a function of that error, aggregation in the NJNITE data, for example, could not be based on number of hours worked by members of treatment and control groups. Similarly, any other outcome variable, such as attrition rate, could not be used as a basis for aggregation since its correlation with sampling variation would induce bias in estimators.

The possible basis for aggregation in the NJNITE data include experimental treatment, city, and ethnicity. For the purposes of relating any of these aggregation variables to each other or to any of the nonaggregation variables, there is essentially no loss of information or precision except from the crudeness of the categories of aggregation (e.g., using three categories of ethnicity rather than 30) if variances and cell n's are provided and distributional assumptions and assumptions about relations among variables are approximated. For relating the unique variables to each other, however, there is certain to be a loss of efficiency. In many cases, there will be no bias accompanying this loss of efficiency, given proper adjustments for the known parameters of aggregation. However, both suppressions of relationships and pseudo relationships are possible in a complex body of data (multifactored in the factor-analysis sense). Consider an extreme example: If variables U_1 and U_2 each were to correlate zero with the variables of aggregation and if a large number of individuals were in each aggregate, then all aggregates would tend to have identical scores on U_1 and identical scores on U_2, and any true relationship between U_1 and U_2 would be suppressed. At the other extreme, if in fact U_1 and U_2 were totally uncorrelated, but if each correlated strongly with some of the variables of aggregation, then an artificial correlation would be generated between them. Obviously, such biases are less the smaller the number of individuals per aggregate, disappearing as this approaches one. Such biases are also less insofar as the variables of aggregation result in a high, all-purpose similarity among the individuals aggregated.

For reasons such as the above, Feige and Watts recommend flexible microaggregation, tailoring the bases used for aggregation so that the efficiency and lack of bias are optimal for the user's needs. Such flexible microaggregation requires that the archiving file have some statistical reanalysis capacity, probably very nearly as much as would be required for doing the customer's analyses internally, releasing only statistical indices (see below). If a user were to sequentially request different microaggregations of the same data, it might be possible to deduce individual data. As discussed more fully below, random deletions of individuals from each microaggregate would protect against this.

Error Inoculation of Individual Data

Boruch (1969; 1971) and others have suggested error inoculation as a means of rendering incriminating responses immune from subpoena. Like the randomized response method (Warner, 1965; Greenberg, et al., 1969; 1970), this was initially proposed for sensitive unique variables, such as drug use or abortion, rather than for public variables usable in decoding individual identity. The present suggested usage is different and has different requirements. (For example, damage from gossip and the threat of blackmail may result from randomly produced misinformation as well as from valid confidential information.) Prior to error inoculation in the release of files for reanalysis, identifiers should of course be eliminated. Most or all public variables should be error inoculated and with enough error so that each individual record contains some imperfection on at least one of the public variables. That is, a potential code-breaker armed with a complete list of all names and public variables should not be able to make any exact matches. Under these conditions, unique variables, even those with sensitive or incriminating information, could be spared error inoculation. All users should be informed of the error inoculation and of its parameters.

Two types of error inoculation can be considered: a) adding random error and b) random score substitution. For a continuous-dimension public variable, such as age, years of education, income (public for some institutions, such as corporations and banks, government employers in some states, as reported for state income tax payments in Wisconsin, etc.), purchase cost of house, mean rental level of residence block, geographic location by latitude and longitude or miles from center of city, etc., a random error of relatively small variance and a mean of zero can be added to each individual score. This increases the overall variance a predictable degree, and attenuates all non-zero relationships (correlation coefficients, regression coefficients, slopes, t ratios, F ratios, etc.) a predictable amount for those relationships where the ordinary linear statistical model holds. The variance of the inoculated error can be kept small relative to the variance of the original data, thus minimally attenuating relationships while effectively maintaining disguise since almost every score is changed to some degree (except for those very few who by chance draw a normal random number of exactly zero). This procedure affects the error of estimation but *not* the degrees of freedom. It does tend to dampen curvilinear relationships, biasing the statistical decision in favor of linear ones. For all public variables whose statistically useful aspects can be converted into continuous form, this is the recommended procedure.

In many data sets, the procedure could be used for most public variables, leaving the remainder with such large cell size (see the discussion of crude report categories for public variables, above) that they could be left without error inoculation. Place of residence and place of birth, for example, could each be replaced by a number of related continuous variables: degree and minutes of longitude and latitude, population per square mile of census tract, percent black of census tract, mean residential rental value of census tract, etc. To each of these variables could be added normal random error (e.g., adding five or ten percent to the variance). If this were done, it might then be unnecessary to add error to high frequency categories, such as sex and race. For low frequency variables that are visibly listed, such as some professions or specialties, a second kind of error inoculation might be necessary.

The second form of error inoculation, random score substitution, is the appropriate procedure for dichotomous variables and for category systems that cannot be converted into continuous dimensions. For example, suppose a sample of doctors contained 30 percent general practitioners, 25 percent internists, 20 percent surgeons, 10 percent gynecologists, 10 percent psychiatrists, and 5 percent other medical specialties. Two randomizations would be involved: first, for each person, a simple random number would be drawn to determine if her or his data were to be left as is or were to be substituted. For example, if a five percent error rate were the aim, all those assigned random numbers from 00 through 04 would be selected for response substitution. For each of these, a second two-digit random number would be selected to determine the substitute response, and this response would be so chosen that the original overall distribution would be maintained. Thus, if the second two-digit random number were between 00 and 29, general practitioner would be assigned; if 30-54, internist; if 55-64, surgeon; etc. (By chance, the substitute specialty would sometimes be the same as the original.)

This method can also be used for continuous variables, but it would be much less desirable than error addition. For tolerable levels of error inoculation, most scores remain exactly the same under random score substitution, making presumptive identification from public variables possible; under the random error addition, most scores are changed to some degree. Under error substitution, the substitute response has no similarity to the correct response, while under normal random error addition, the response is still similar to the original data, big errors are much less frequent than small ones, and thus much information is still retained. Even so, the general effect of the error inoculation by response substitution on summary statistics of association is calculable although statistical power is inevitably reduced. (For error inoculation of statistical products rather than individual data, see below.)

In summary, error inoculation of individual data on public variables, while costly as far as statistical efficiency is concerned, is an acceptable safeguard that still permits many valuable reanalyses to be done.

In-file Capacity to Run Outsiders' Statistical Analyses

It is already the practice of some archives of research data to provide for reanalysis of their data, not by releasing the raw data, but instead by performing on their data the statistical analyses requested by an outsider, who is charged for the costs involved. Project Talent, the American Council on Education, the Bureau of the Census, the STATPAK service of Statistics Canada, and other repositories provide such services. One of the obviously desirable features of maximally useful federal data archives would be that each be provided with such statistical analysis capacity. It is also in the interest of increasing our capacity to evaluate federal programs that non-governmental archives with large relevant record sets be funded with federal evaluation research funds. Blue Cross/Blue Shield and other carriers of medical insurance, automobile and life insurance companies, etc., all could be made accessible by funding each major record center with a statistician and a computer programmer for this purpose.

Where the requested outputs are summary statistics, such as means, standard deviations, correlation coefficients, regression weights, slopes, rates, etc., summarized over large populations, few if any threats to individual privacy are involved. For sample surveys, the lists of participants can and should be kept confidential, precluding most conceivable code-breaking efforts. Where the data represent a complete census of some small population and where an outside user is able to request repeatedly separate analyses, he or she might be able to decode data on a single person by using knowledge of public variables to move that person from one cell to another in two subsequent analyses, keeping the other people intact, and thus learn that one person's data by subtraction. If this is a hazard, the precaution of deleting one or more persons at random from each cell (deleting different persons for each reanalysis) will preclude such a subtractive code-breaking.

Where the output requested involves frequency counts and where, as in complete censuses, knowledge of who is in the file is available, the anonymity-breaking possibilities are much greater. The problem is the same as is met with in the publication of detailed tabulations. Hansen (1971) describes as "random modification" an approach to altering exact count data prior to publication. To adjust counts within categories, one simply multiplies the count by a random factor whose range is, say, 0.5-1.5 and whose properties are known. The long-run average count will be accurate if the random number is drawn from a uniform distribution, but the variance of the published estimators will be large relative to unadulterated counts. The method differs from error inoculation in that modification is limited to published count data and is not introduced at the individual data level. Where the outside analyst has no access to individual records, but does have access to tabulated statistical data, the Hansen variant appears to be more desirable than error inoculation of individual data.

Members of the Statistics Canada staff have recommended "random rounding" for the preservation of privacy in the publication of tabular material and in performing customer-specified analyses. Felligi and Phillips (1974) provide a convenient introduction to the papers that various members of this group have published. Even if small cell frequencies--say, below three--are not reported, these can usually be reconstructed from marginal frequencies and from considering several tables jointly. Collapsing categories into cruder ones must be applied to all tables involving that dimension if reconstruction of small cell frequencies is to be precluded, and thus has a greater informational cost than random rounding. Ordinary rounding is biased through a preponderance of rounding down and, because of its fixed rules, also often permits reconstruction of the real frequencies.

In random rounding, all cell frequencies are rounded, either up or down depending on the random number drawn. Were the true frequency exactly half way between the rounded values (e.g., even multiples of five), then the chances of rounding up or down would be 50-50. In their system, as the true frequency is nearer the rounding up value, the chances of drawing a rounding up are increased so that an average of many roundings will give the true value. Marginals and total are rounded independently of cell roundings. Corresponding sums and averages are computed so as to be consistent both with the rounded frequencies and with the actual average per unit values computed on the unrounded data. Fellegi and Phillips report minimal bias or information loss once frequencies rise above 10 or 15 persons.

INTERFILE EXCHANGE OF CONFIDENTIAL DATA

The second major category of use to be considered is that in which statistical relations are sought between the data contained in two confidential files. In accordance with this paper's objective of providing very conservative but usable procedures, this can be achieved without increasing the number of file personnel or users who have access to confidential information about individuals. That is, if File A is being related to File B, the custodians of File A need not end up with confidential information from File B, or vice versa. Neither file need expand in the amount of confidential information it contains.

Even under these restrictions, interfile exchange is an extremely valuable tool in federal agency evaluation research. Once the major administrative archives of government, insurance companies, hospitals, etc., are organized and staffed for such research, the amount of interpretable outcome data on ameliorative programs can be increased tenfold.

For example, Fischer (1972) reports on the use of income tax data in a follow-up on the effectiveness of manpower training programs. While these data are not perfect or complete for the evaluation of such a training program, they are highly relevant. Claims on unemployment compensation and welfare payments would also be relevant. Cost is an important advantage. Using a different approach, Heller (1972) reports retrieval costs of $1 per person for a study of several thousand trainees. Even if $10 were more realistic, these costs are to be compared with costs of $100 or more per interview in individual follow-up interviews with ex-trainees. Rate of retrieval is another potential advantage. Follow-up interviews in urban manpower training programs have failed to locate as many as 50 percent of the population, and 30 percent loss rates would be common. Differential loss rates for experimental and control groups are also common, with the control groups less motivated to continue. In the NJNITE, over three years, 25.3 percent of the controls were lost, compared with a loss of only 6.5 percent of those in the most remunerative experimental condition. While retrieval rates overall might be no higher for withholding tax records, the differential bias in cooperation would probably be avoided, and the absence of data could be interpreted, with caution, as the absence of such earnings.

In many settings where programs are focused on special needs and where there are more eligible applicants than there are spaces for them, access to government records can enable program administrators to use experimental evaluation designs at minimal costs. With an excess of eligible applicants, there are several strategies available. An administrator can randomly select trainees from the pool of eligibles or from a pool of those at the borderline of eligibility, keeping records on those randomly rejected as a control group. Or the administrator can quantify the grounds of eligibility or some component of it, admitting those who are most eligible according to this quantitative criterion and keeping records on those above and below the cut-off point as categorized by their eligibility scores. Access to appropriate administrative file records for subsequent outcome studies then provides a low-cost estimate of program effects. Such results might be used to justify an expensive follow-up by individual interviews.

The requirements for achieving such linkage are more complicated than for intrafile reanalysis. But it can and has been done with adequate guards to confidentiality (e.g., Schwartz and Orleans, 1967; Fischer, 1972). Even though such use requires special restrictions and rituals, its potential value justifies an investment in making these procedures routinely available. In what follows, four procedures are discussed: (1) microaggregation; (2) synthetic linkage by matching; (3) link file brokerage; and (4) mutually insulated file linkage. We provide no discussion of the procedures for file merging because the number of situations in which full confidentiality protection of all data from subpoena, etc., is presently available to both of the federal agencies that might be involved in a file merger is extremely rare. If two agencies do have such full protection, adequate within-agency procedures would be available to protect merged files, including a need-to-know access limitation for agency employees.

Microaggregation

While the focus of the Feige and Watts (1970) paper is on single file analyses (albeit for a unified confidential federal statistical data center), their paper suggests that files be linked after microaggregation by parallel use of the same aggregation criteria, for example, one based on geographical units--a "micro zip-code system" (p. 270). For administrative files, this would certainly be of great use. For example, to have average income data available on pseudo census tracts or block statistics (subject to limitations on the minimum number of individuals within aggregates) would greatly expand our capacity for social reality testing. If social experiments in community services or urban renewal could be allocated by census tract or block, microaggregated administrative data would be available for program evaluation.

Such a system could not be used to link NJNITE data to census or income tax records, for example, since the treatment was not assigned by microregion. It would be usable only for those social experiments where the experimental units corresponded to census tracts, blocks, zip codes, or other compact aggregation bases in use by other files. Moreover, even in such cases, the treatment would have to saturate the area, being applied to most persons in the aggregation unit rather than just to a few selected ones. Such experiments will occur, and this method should be kept in mind. But for most federal agency evaluation research, useful interfile linkage will have to be achieved through individual identifiers.

Synthetic Linkage by Matching

This title will be used to designate a technique used by Budd and Radner (1969), Okner (1972; 1974), and others (Ruggles and Ruggles, 1974; Alter, 1974) to link the data in two files from which individual identifiers have been removed or which contain only similar individuals, not necessarily the same individuals. If there are a number of variables shared by both files, these can be used for a one-to-one matching of individual cases from which a composite individual file can be made combining the unique data of the two files. These extended files can then be analyzed as though all of the data came from the same person.

Let us call the shared variables $X_1, X_2, \ldots X_n$, the variables unique to the first file $Y_1, Y_2 \ldots Y_n$, and those unique to the second file $Z_1, Z_2 \ldots Z_n$. A typical analytic goal is to determine relationships between Y and Z variables. If the X and Y variables and/or the X and Z variables are entirely independent, any Y and Z relationships will be lost, inasmuch as an essentially random matching will have been achieved. Consideration of the effect of error and other unique variance in variables would seem to predict that even with strong X-Y and X-Z relationships, the Y-Z correlations will be underestimated since they will be attenuated not only with the unique variance of the Y and Z variables (as in a direct study) but also by the unique variance in the X variables used for matching. The extent of such underestimation will be a function of the exactness of the matching and of the two multiple correlations between the matching X variables as independent variables and the specific Y and Z variables as dependent variables. It is possible that the extent of such attenuation can be estimated.

Where the two files differ widely on the means of the X variables--as where, for example, a survey of unemployed youth were to be linked with census data or, as in an example mentioned by Okner (1974), where homeowners were matched with non-homeowners, both from IRS files--the matching process will systematically undermatch for the latent variables underlying this difference and for other indicators in Y and Z symptomatic of these latent variables (as per considerations of the theory of error in variables and the experience with regression artifacts). Even with no file population mean differences to begin with (as he had two sample surveys of the same population), Alter (1974) found that inexact matches were necessary and that these cumulated to produce significant differences, even on the X variables used in matching. For other criticisms, see Sims (1972; 1974). The technique is still under evaluation. Its practitioners are properly self-critical. We may soon expect trial runs where all variables, X, Y, and Z, exist in the same file so that the Y-Z relationship produced by matching linkage can be compared with the true values. For the present, we judge the technique inferior to linkage procedures (such as the mutually insulated file linkage discussed below) based on indivdual identity and using individual identifiers, if these are available.

Synthetic linkage by matching would not seem feasible for the specific purpose of using administrative archives for follow-up measures in the evaluation of the effects of experimental programs.

Link File Brokerage

Manniche and Hayes (1957), Astin and Boruch (1970), and others have proposed that a responsible broker, located perhaps in another country, provide the linkage. Domestically, we can visualize this done in an agency like the Census Bureau, where records are immune from subpoena. Each file would prepare a list of names or other individual identifiers and corresponding file-specific code numbers, which would be turned over to the linkage broker. Using the individual identifiers common to the two files, the broker would prepare a list, deck, or tape linking the two file-specific codes from which the names and other individual identifiers would be removed. Subsequently, the files would provide data sets to the broker identified only by file-specific codes. The broker could then merge such decks from the two files and turn the merged deck over to either of the files, with both file-specific codes now deleted.

This suggestion comes out of a well-justified policy of keeping the data of a research project separated, insofar as possible, from the names and addresses of the respondents during data analysis. But it also assumes that deletion of identifiers provides adequate protection of confidentiality. As we have seen, this is not always sufficient. In addition, the broker represents a new file that has access to identified confidential information (unless it can be assured that the two lists linking public identifiers to the file-specific code information were destroyed immediately after use).

As originally proposed, link file brokerage also permits personal identifiers to be reconnected easily with the total merged data set if either of the original files still has its original data with personal identifiers. The replication of the unique variables on both the original data and on the new composite deck will usually provide a basis for exact matching, making the reinstatement of personal identifiers on the merged deck a simple process and thus giving one file access to the confidential information of the other file.

To avoid these difficulties, the link file brokerage device must be modified in one or more directions. In some settings it might be possible for each original file to destroy all records of names and other public identifiers after having transmitted the linking list to the broker. This would be hard to police, and particularly hard for one file to insure on the part of the other file, as would be necessary in settings where a custodian of confidential data has assumed responsibility for restricting the dissemination of the data in individually identifiable form. Where the broker is isolated from opportunities and temptations to misuse data, or if ways can be developed to guarantee the broker's destruction of the intermediate lists containing identifiers, it would be desirable for the broker to do the analyses on the merged deck, operating as a public utility data archive, as described in a preceding section. (Such analyses could be done without the broker knowing the meaning of the variables being analyzed, although later publication could reveal variable names.) Under such conditions, the merged deck would never get back to the original files. If the merged deck is to be shared with an originating file, sufficient error inoculation of the unique variables could preclude the exact matching that would reinstate identifiers.

The use of a link file broker may be of some value in protecting against subpoena if the broker is located beyond the reach of subpoena or protected from subpoena by statute. But, for the goal of restricting identifiable data to the files for which permission has been given, this system has serious weaknesses unless much modified.

(The linking of research files by remembered or regenerated codes retained by the respondent so that longitudinal studies are made possible while files have no individual identifiers is a separate technique needing a review and analysis. Where one of the files is a government record, this does not seem feasible.)

Mutually Insulated File Linkage

This phrase is used to cover a group of similar devices for linking files without merging, preserving confidentiality. The essential notions involved have no doubt been hit upon independently on many occasions, particularly in statistical research with government records. Of published discussions, probably the first and certainly the most cited is by Schwartz and Orleans (1967), in a study linking public opinion survey responses to income tax returns. But it is clear from Fischer (1972) that similar processes have been in use in a number of government agencies.

It seems well to start with a concrete exposition of the full model in its most conservative version, and subsequently to discuss alternatives and abbreviations. The hypothetical problem in Figure 1 is to relate a local Job Corps experimental program to Social Security Administration records on earnings subject to FICA deductions. It is assumed that both files are to be kept confidential from each other. The experimental trainees and the control trainees would have been grouped by socio-economic level, chosen as a useful dimension of analysis. Where there are a sufficient number of trainees within a given level, two or more lists would have been formed. The resulting 26 lists would then have been assigned list names from A to Z on a random basis. Each list itself would consist solely of person identifiers useful in SSA's retrieval operation, such as name and Social Security number. SSA would delete one person at random from each list, locate the data on all variables of interest for the remainder, compute for each variable a mean, variance, and

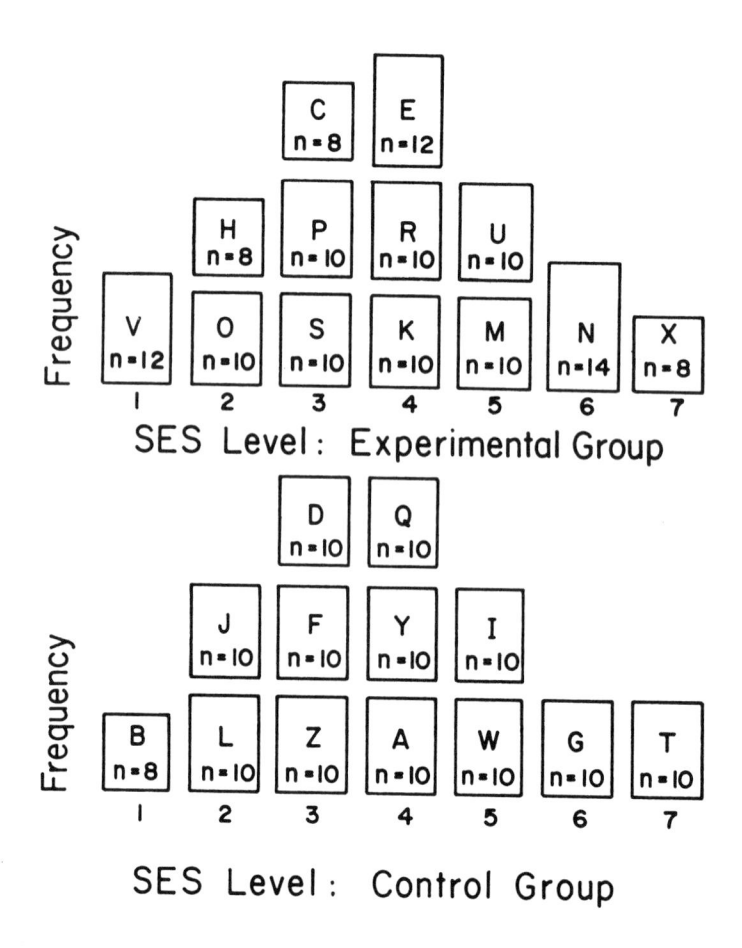

FIGURE 1 Hypothetical data from two treatment groups in a social experiment, grouped by SES level and given coded list designators A through Z.

frequency for the persons on the list for whom FICA deductions were on record, and send back these summary statistics, identified with their unique list designators. The Job Corps project evaluators would then reassemble these cell-by-cell data into their meaningful dimensional order and compute summary statistics. While the SSA file would get individual identifiers, they would get no interpretable data about these individuals. In return, they would send back no information about individuals, but only summary statistics about a group, which the evaluators would decode as a data cell in a statistical grid. The returned data would be microaggregated, but by an aggregation scheme unrevealed to and undecodable by the SSA. It should be emphasized that the researching agency receiving the microaggregated data (in this example, the Job Corps) must not in its published report provide results for any single list, but must further aggregate the dependent-variable information received from the furnishing agency (SSA) in such a manner as to conceal the confidential characteristics of the individuals for whom the information might be sought. Otherwise, publication of the furnished information by the researching agency could provide the furnishing agency with the ability to identify the individuals in terms of the independent variables by which they are characterized.

In Figure 1, the vertical dimension represents frequency, but it could represent cross-classification on any other dimensional score. Note that adjacent (and even identical) scale values are assigned haphazardly non-adjacent list codes. Not only are the names of the variables disguised from the second file, but also the ordering of respondents on these variables. When the cell means and variances have been returned to the initiating file, they can be reassembled to provide publishable group means, standard deviations, t ratios, F ratios, covariances, correlations, regression weights, slopes, etc. Frequency distributions, cross tabulations, and cell means would often reveal to the second file (SSA) first file (Job Corps) information, although this might be precluded by adding random values as discussed by Hansen (1971) and above.

It probably would have been of both scientific and public policy value to have the results of the NJNITE cross-validated with SSA income data, ideally using years prior to, during, and subsequent to the three years of the experiment. As a hypothetical exercise, consideration of such a study will serve to develop a number of points. While not all income would be picked up in this manner, the results would still be very useful. The effects of attrition, and especially differential attrition, would be minimized, since many non-cooperators in the periodic interviews would still have employers sending in reports to the SSA on earnings subject to FICA. For such a study to be done, lists would be prepared subject to the same considerations discussed under the first presentation of microaggregation above. Thus, each of the eight experimental payment plans in each of the five cities would provide 40 lists of varying size, averaging some 16 persons per list. The control subjects in each of the five cities could be randomly assigned to eight lists per city. The resulting 80 lists of names would be randomly assigned list designations and then sent to the SSA.

With these uses and procedures in mind, some more detailed problems and questions can be considered.

1. The random deletion of one individual from each list is to prevent detection of identified individual data through repeated negotiations. For

example, without that precaution, File A could group an individual in one list on one negotiation and delete that individual from the list on a second negotiation, keeping all of the other individuals on the list intact. The difference between the two means would then represent this individual's score. The random deletion process prevents this possibility and would, of course, be done anew for each negotiation.

In place of random deletion, the addition of a random normal error to each set of scores for each list could be substituted. In the case of longitudinal data, this would seem to be more damaging to the analysis than the loss of one randomly selected case per list.

2. In the Schwartz and Orleans study (1967), individual scores were provided, rather than means and variances. This was adequate safeguard in that instance, but where repeated negotiation between files has to be anticipated, it would usually permit disclosure of individual data by the device of moving a person from one list to another list on successive negotiations. A random deletion from each list would not usually protect against this.

If the general normal linear additive model is being assumed in the analysis, the cell means and variances are as useful as the individual scores, although new computational versions of standard formulas are needed. Other summary statistics, higher order moments, indices of skewness, etc., could be added to the mean and variance data.

An intermediate degree of disguise can be considered, in which the originating file turns over its variables with code names for the variables (rather than, as here suggested, unique and scrambled codes for each category on each variable). This probably makes the discovery of the variable more likely and makes it definitely possible once the results are published, if the second file has kept the records of the transaction. In contrast, under mutually insulated file linkage as first presented above, the published analyses of the data by the initiating file would provide summary statistics for the whole sample, pooling the information from numerous lists, so that the second file would not be able to identify values on the variables reported in the published articles for any lists they might retain.

4. Lower limits on the number of persons in any list need to be established by practical exercises in identity breaking. Heller (1972) says only "small cells have to be withheld." Fischer (1972) suggests a three-person minimum. The random deletion of one person per cell gets very costly at this cell size. In the illustrations above, a minimum of eight has been used.

5. The requirement of minimal cell size will set limits on the number of variables or dimensions from the originating file that can be employed. One, two, or three may be common maximums. (There is no limit, however, on the number of variables from the second file.) More first-file variables can be handled by repeated negotiations. If, as for a factor analysis, one wanted to relate 20 variables from the first file with 20 from the second, one might do this in seven negotiations, each using two or three variables from File 1 and all 20 from File 2, to get the 400 cross-file correlations. The 90 intra-File 1 and the 90 intra-File 2 correlations would best be done within each file, but for the linked cases pooled from all lists. (For File 1 to do the File 2 intrafile correlations from the list aggregates it has received would potentially bias these correlations as described under microaggregation above.) The matrix of correlations would have the defect of being based upon differing

numbers of cases, but with substantial numbers this should not render a factor analysis inconsistent.

6. Because of some confusion in previous discussions of the method, it must be emphasized that the file linkage achieved is strictly limited and that file merging does not result. File 2 gets no addition at all. File 1 has access to File 2 variables for further analyses only in a microaggregated form; that is, File 1 could microaggregate other File 1 variables by the lists used in a prior negotiation and could relate these means to the means on the File 2 variables received in that prior negotiation. These indirectly estimated relations would not be ascertained with the precision of those involving variables used in the initial negotiations, but rather in the form described for the relationships among unique variables ascertained from microaggregate data, as described in the first section above.

7. In the hypothetical illustration involving the NJNITE, SSA rather than IRS files were used because consideration of the latter raises several unique issues that would unduly complicate the general model. First, there are some interfile exchange settings where it is a loss of privacy and a breach of confidentiality for one file to even inform another file that a person exists. If the NJNITE were to send its lists to the IRS, this might make the IRS aware of non-filers who should have been filing income tax returns. To avoid this, the NJNITE would need to access the IRS index files, identify the tax return document locator numbers for those who had filed returns and negotiate only for summary information for filers (e.g., Steinberg and Pritzker, 1969). This is probably not a realistic worry for the NJNITE because most of its respondents were probably motivated to file tax returns in order to obtain refunds of withheld taxes. However, even if any exposed delinquent cases would likely be cases in which the IRS owed the wage earner money rather than vice versa, the best approach would still be to have the NJNITE access the IRS index files. In many studies there would be a real jeopardy, and however the researcher felt about delinquent taxpayers, she or he would realize that it was not a part of the research role to bring them to justice and would therefore arrange for screening by her or his own staff so that negotiations with the IRS would be limited to known tax filers.

Schwartz and Orleans (1967), working with prosperous respondents, avoided this problem by a three-stage negotiation. First, the IRS provided them with a regionally concentrated list of names and addresses of taxpayers who itemized their deductions and filled out their own income tax forms. Four groups to receive four different types of interview were randomly chosen. These were further subclassified by the attitudes they expressed and formed into lists that were sent to IRS in the second stage. In the third stage, the IRS turned back to Schwartz and Orleans unidentified data in scrambled order within lists. In that instance they published data that identified only the treatment groups. If, however, they had published information concerning attitudes or behavior, the protection of privacy would have required further aggregation, as mentioned above. The first stage could also be done by asking respondents whether or not they filed income tax returns or by ascertaining withholding tax status by knowing their place of work, etc. In the three-way linkage study discussed by Steinberg and Pritzker (1969), the IRS allowed a Census Bureau representative to examine the IRS taxpayer index to find out if there were tax records on certain respondents, but the representative was not allowed to see the content of the records. Only for those Census Bureau cases certified to exist in IRS files were tax data requested. Use of this device, or the stage one of Schwartz and Orleans, depends upon the relative sensitivity of the knowledge of presence or absence of persons in each of the files; this must be evaluated separately for each study.

8. Considering a hypothetical NJNITE-IRS exchange also raises the possibility that in some cases co-occurrence on a File 1 list might provide meaningful incriminating evidence to File 2. For example, suppose that NJNITE income supplement recipients were supposed to report this experimental income on their tax forms and that most of them had done so. The IRS's general knowledge of the experiment, plus their observation that on certain lists many persons were reporting such income, could have led them to suspect that the others on such lists should also have done so.

Such possibilities occur when the second file has partial information on a variable being used in the negotiation by the first file. Such information leads the second file to deduce a dimension of homogeneity for the list (lists must be homogeneous for the system to work). This deduction then justifies the deduction that the remaining persons on the list should also have the same value on this variable. In general, this is a very unlikely set of circumstances and would not stand in the way of most interfile exchanges. But it is an appropriate worry in this concrete case, and it should be checked. Consideration should be given to a procedure that has been used which requires embedding the File 1 population in a larger one. Random subsets would include one or more non-File 1 population members in each microaggregated list. Other lists would contain small numbers of the File 1 population and the largest portion from the larger population. This, while more expensive, creates the desired heterogeneity. In carrying out analyses using File 2 data, File 1 could discard lists primarily from the larger population. Occasionally, concerns about list homogeneity will lead one to forego a dimension of analysis. One might decide not to use lists grouped on criminal record, or grouped on having committed a given crime, because of the danger that co-listing will convey incriminating information.

For most of the wide range of federal agency evaluation research uses, such incriminating categories will not be involved. Classifying Job Corps trainees by number of months of training will produce no co-listing jeopardy with either the IRS or the SSA. If family income provides jeopardy when negotiating for IRS or welfare agency records, this variable can be sacrificed and some effects of the training still ascertained, providing that there has been a good experimental or quasi-experimental scheduling of admissions.

SUMMARY

Realistic testing of the effects of federal programs designed to ameliorate social problems can be greatly improved by making available administrative records on unemployment, earnings, educational attainment, medical insurance usage, and the like. Research data evaluating social experiments need to be open to critical reanalysis. Both types of use of records and files must be done in ways that avoid violating the confidentiality of the data provided by respondents or increasing the risk of gossip, blackmail, or arrest. Confidentiality-preserving modes of access to files and to interfile exchange for statistical analysis exist. It is in the public interest that facilities for using these modes of access be made readily available. Where maximal protection of confidentiality is required, the present analysis of the problem results in the following conclusions:

1. The major sets of administrative and research records on individuals can be kept separate, rather than being merged into combined data banks, and still permit useful statistical linkage.

2. It would be desirable that data archives relevant to federal agency program evaluation be funded to do statistical analyses on their own data. Data files relevant to federal program evaluation include not only governmental records such as Census Bureau, Social Security, Internal Revenue, crime, and welfare, but also record files in the private sector such as medical and automobile insurance.

3. In order for statistical analyses to be done that link data from different files, all files should record common person identifiers, such as name, birth date, birth place, and Social Security number. In the mode of mutually insulated interfile linkage described here, the presence of such shared identifiers does not jeopardize confidentiality. The confidential information linked with each personal identifier remains limited to the original file.

4. For the statistical reanalysis of data from a single file, it is usually not a complete safeguard to release the data with personal identification deleted. If, in the data released, there are items of information that are also available publicly, then additional precautions are required, such as restrictions on the number and refinement of these public variables in the data released or error inoculation of the public variables. Microaggregated release is acceptable. The optimal procedure is for the file in question to have the capacity to do the required reanalyses itself, using randomized rounding where frequency data are released.

5. For the interfile exchange of confidential data, where one or both of the files are confidential, analysts should actively consider use of mutually insulated file linkage with random deletions of one person per list. It would be desirable that all relevant files be staffed with the minimum retrieval and statistical analysis capacities required to cooperate in any such linkage.

BIBLIOGRAPHY*

Alter, H. E. 1974. Creation of a synthetic data set by linking records of the Canadian Survey of Consumer Finances with the Family Expenditure Survey 1970. *Annals of Economic and Social Measurement* 3:373-94.

Astin, A. W., and Boruch, R. F. 1970. A link file system for assuring confidentiality in longitudinal studies. *American Educational Research Journal* 1:615-24.

Bauman, R. A., David, M. H., and Miller, R. F. 1970. Working with complex data files: II. The Wisconsin assets and incomes studies archive. In *Data bases, computers, and the social sciences*, pp. 112-36. Edited by R. L. Bisco. New York: Wiley-Interscience.

Boruch, R. F. 1969. Educational research and the confidentiality of data: A case study. *ACE Research Reports* (4). Washington, D. C.: American Council on Education.

Boruch, R. F. 1971. Maintaining confidentiality in educational research: A systematic analysis. *American Psychologist* 26:413-30.

Boruch, R. F. 1972. Strategies for eliciting and merging confidential social research data. *Policy Sciences* 3:275-97.

Boruch, R. F. 1972a. Relations among statistical methods for assuring confidentiality of data. *Social Science Research* 1:403-14.

Bryant, E. C. and Hansen, M. H. Invasion of privacy and surveys: A growing dilemma. Paper presented at the Smithsonian-Navy Conference on Survey Alternatives, Santa Fe, New Mexico, April 22-24, 1975.

Budd, E. C., and Radner, D. B. 1969. The O. B. E. size distribution series: Methods and tentative results for 1964. *The American Economic Review* 59:435-49.

Dunn, E. S., Jr. 1974. *Social information processing and statistical systems: Change and reform.* New York: Wiley-Interscience.

Feige, E. L., and Watts, H. W. 1970. Protection of privacy through micro-aggregation. In *Data bases, computers, and the social sciences*. Edited by R. L. Bisco. New York: Wiley-Interscience.

Fellegi, I. P. 1972. On the question of statistical confidentiality. *Journal of the American Statistical Association* 67:7-18.

Fellegi, I. P., and Phillips, J. L. 1974. Statistical confidentiality: Some theory and applications to data dissemination. *Annals of Economic and Social Measurement* 3:399-409.

---

*This list contains some items that have not been specifically cited in the paper.

Fischer, J. L. 1972. The uses of Internal Revenue Service data. In *Evaluating the impact of manpower programs*, pp. 177-80. Edited by M. E. Borus. Lexington, Mass.: D. C. Heath.

Goslin, D. A. 1971. Ethical and legal aspects of the collection and use of educational information. In *Proceedings of the 1970 invitational Conference on Testing Problems*, pp. 149-59. Edited by G. V. Glass. Princeton, N. J.: Educational Testing Service.

Greenberg, B. G., Abul-Ela, A. A., Simon, W. R., and Horvitz, D. G. 1969. The unrelated question randomized response model: Theoretical framework. *Journal of the American Statistical Association* 64:520-39.

Greenberg, B. G., Abernathy, J. R., and Horvitz, D. G. 1970. A new survey technique and its application in the field of public health. *Milbank Memorial Fund Quarterly* 68(4, Part 2):39-55.

Hansen, M. H. 1971. Insuring confidentiality of individual records in data storage and retrieval for statistical purposes. In *Federal Statistics*, Vol. II, *Report of the President's Commission*, pp. 48-61. Washington, D. C.: U. S. Government Printing Office (No. 4000-0269).

Heller, R. N. 1972. The uses of social security administration data. In *Evaluating the impact of manpower programs*, pp. 197-201. Edited by M. E. Borus. Lexington, Mass.: D. C. Heath.

Hoffman, L. J., ed. 1973. *Security and privacy in computer systems*. Los Angeles: Melville (Wiley).

Hoffman, L. J., and Miller, W. F. 1970. How to obtain a personal dossier from a data bank. *Datamation* 16:74-5.

Hunt, M. K. and Turn, R. 1974. *Privacy and security in data bank systems: An annotated bibliography, 1970-1973*. Santa Monica: The Rand Corporation.

Kershaw, D. N. 1972. A negative income tax experiment. *Scientific American* 227:19-25.

Kershaw, D. N. 1974. The New Jersey negative income tax experiment: A summary of the design, operations and results of the first large-scale social science experiment. Dartmouth/OECD Seminar on "Social Research and Public Policies," September 13-15, 1974.

Manniche, E., and Hayes, D. P. 1957. Respondent anonymity and data matching. *Public Opinion Quarterly* 21:384-88.

Miller, A. R. 1971. *The assault on privacy*. Ann Arbor, Mich.: University of Michigan Press.

Okner, B. A. 1972. Constructing a new data base from existing microdata sets: The 1966 merge file. *Annals of Economic and Social Measurement* 1:325-42.

Okner, B. A. 1974. Data matching and merging: An overview. *Annals of Economic and Social Measurement* 3:347-52.

Riecken, H. W., Boruch, R. F., Campbell, D. T., Caplan, N., Glennan, T. K., Pratt, J., Rees, A., and Williams, W. 1974. *Social experimentation: A method for planning and evaluating social intervention*. New York: Academic Press.

Ruebhausen, O. M., and Brim, O. G., Jr. 1965. Privacy and behavioral research. *Columbia Law Review* 65:1184-211.

Ruggles, N., and Ruggles, R. 1974. A strategy for merging and matching microdata sets. *Annals of Economic and Social Measurement* 3:353-71.

Russell Sage Foundation. 1970. *Guidelines for the collection, maintenance and dissemination of pupil records*. New York: Russell Sage Foundation.

Sawyer, J., and Schechter, H. 1968. Computers, privacy, and the National Data Center: The responsibility of social scientists. *American Psychologist* 23:810-18.

Scheuren, F., Bridges, B., and Kilss, B. Subsampling the current population survey: 1963 pilot link study. Report No. 1: *Studies from interagency data linkages*. Washington, D. C.: U. S. Department of Health, Education, and Welfare, Social Security Administration, Office of Research and Statistics, August 1973. (DHEW Pub. No. (SSA) 74-11750.)

Schwartz, R. D. and Orleans, S. 1967. On legal sanctions. *University of Chicago Law Review* 34:274-300.

Sims, C. A. "Comments" to Okner's 1966 merge file. 1972. *Annals of Economic and Social Measurement* 1:343-45.

Sims, C. A. 1974. Comment: January 17, 1974. *Annals of Economic and Social Measurement* 3:395-97.

Steinberg, J. Interacting data systems and the measurement of income size distributions. Paper presented to the Conference on Research in Income and Wealth: The Size Distribution of Income and Wealth, University of Pennsylvania, March 1967. (To be published.)

Steinberg, J. Some observations on linkage of survey and administrative record data. *Studies from interagency data linkages*. Washington, D. C.: U. S. Department of Health, Education, and Welfare, Social Security Administration, Office of Research and Statistics, August 1973. (DHEW Pub. No. (SSA) 74-11750.)

Steinberg, J., and Pritzker, L. 1969. Some experiences with the reflections on data linkage in the United States. *Bulletin of the International Statistical Institute* 42:786-805.

Turn, R. 1973. *Privacy transformations for data bank systems*. Rand Research Report P-4955. Santa Monica, Calif.: Rand Corporation.

Ware, W. H., et al. *Records, computers, and the rights of citizens*. Report of the Secretary's Advisory Committee on Automated Personal Data Systems, U. S. Department of Health, Education, and Welfare, July 1973. Washington, D. C.: U. S. Government Printing Office, No. 1700-00116.

Warner, S. L. 1965. Randomized response: A survey technique for eliminating evasive answer bias. *Journal of the American Statistical Association* 60:63-69.

Watts, H. W. 1972. Microdata: Lessons from the SEO and the Graduated Work Incentive Experiment. *Economic and Social Measurement* 1:183-92.

Watts, H. W., and Rees, A., eds. 1973. *Final report of the New Jersey Graduated Work Incentive Experiment*. Volume I. *An overview of the labor supply results and of Central labor-supply results* (700 pp.). Volume II. *Studies relating to the validity and generalizability of the results* (250 pp.). Volume III. *Response with respect to expenditure, health, and social behavior and technical notes* (300 pp.). Madison, Wisc.: Institute for Research on Poverty, University of Wisconsin. (Duplicated.)

Westin, A. F. 1967. *Privacy and freedom*. New York: Antheum.

Westin, A. F., ed. 1971. *Information technology in a democracy*. Cambridge: Harvard University Press.

Westin, A. F. 1972. *Data banks in a free society*. New York: Quadrangle Books.
Wheeler, S., ed. 1969. *Files and dossiers in American life*. New York: Russell Sage Foundation.

APPENDIX B

A RESEARCHER'S SHIELD STATUTE:

GUARDING AGAINST THE COMPULSORY DISCLOSURE OF RESEARCH DATA

Paul Nejelski
Director, Institute of Judicial Administration
New York University Law School. L.L.B. Yale, 1962

Howard Peyser
Research Associate
J.D. New York University, 1974

TABLE OF CONTENTS

INTRODUCTION	B- 1
SUMMARY	B- 4
AN ACT TO PROTECT RESEARCHERS AND THEIR SUBJECTS	B- 9
COMMENTARY	B-12
THE NEED FOR STATUTORY PROTECTION	B-12
THE POWER TO LEGISLATE	B-26
COVERAGE: PEOPLE	B-31
MATERIAL COVERED	B-35
SCOPE OF PROTECTION: POSSIBLE LIMITATIONS	B-41
PROCEDURAL ISSUES	B-55
WAIVER	B-58
REFERENCES AND NOTES	B-62

INTRODUCTION

The need for a statute to protect researchers from the compulsory disclosure of their data has only recently been a concern to the research community and the public at large. Scientific inquiry based on the collection of information about research subjects is as old as the scientific method itself. However, the scale and scope of this inquiry in recent years has increased dramatically. As a result of methodologies that rely heavily on interviews and observations, the researcher has become the repository of large amounts of information potentially useful for purposes other than scientific inquiry, such as use in a criminal trial by either prosecution or defense.

The variety of parties who have an interest in a statute guarding against the compulsory disclosure of research data makes it difficult to analyze the issues involved. At least seven such parties have been identified.[1]

Research <u>subjects</u> have paramount interest in keeping the invasion of their privacy to a minimum and making sure that the information they supply will not be the basis for prosecution or reprisal. <u>Researchers</u> have a complementary interest in being able to assure their subjects that the information they provide will be confidential; they will thus be able to elicit candid, sensitive, and personal responses. Researchers also have an interest in making sure that, once the information is supplied, it is not used for purposes other than their research. For example, researchers who are investigating criminal activity do not want to become an arm of law enforcement agencies. If they feel that their data will be so used, they may refrain from the research activity.

The <u>sponsor</u>, the agency that provides the funds for the research, and the <u>facilitator</u>, the agency by which the researcher is given access to subjects and records, both have an interest in the quality of the results of the research. Because the quality of research is directly dependent upon the researchers' ability and willingness to elicit information from their subjects, these two parties have a stake in the protection provided by the proposed statute. To the extent that the <u>state</u>[2] assumes the role of the sponsor or facilitator, it, too, has an interest in assuring against the compelled disclosure of research data. One caveat, however, is that in a free society immunity against compulsory disclosure of research data should not be used by the state as a cloak for hiding information from the public.

The <u>requesting party</u>, attempting to compel the researcher to disclose information, also has an interest in protecting research data from subpoena or other legal process. Compulsory disclosure of information will yield this party immediate information. The resultant inhibition of research activity will, however, decrease the useful research data available to the requesting party in the long run.

<u>Society</u> at large has an enormous interest in the fruits of research dependent upon assurances against compulsory disclosure of data. In providing valuable research in such diverse areas as drug abuse control, the study of American sexual practices, and formulating intelligent foreign policy, the research process has implicitly depended upon the fact that information supplied would not be subject to compulsory legal process.

Interest in protecting against abuses of the collection and dissemination of research data has been highlighted by several recent developments. The similar dilemma of protecting journalists' sources and information has received wide public recognition and been the subject of frequent litigation. Researchers themselves have for the first time been subpoenaed to reveal their data, resulting in the search for new modes of protection. Increased governmental involvement in research, especially through large-scale patronage or mandatory evaluation of its programs, has led to special problems.

The statute proposed here resolves the competing interests in favor of safeguarding the research process. It is drafted in terms of federal protection for researchers in both federal and state proceedings. The statute broadly defines the individuals and the types of data protected. While the statute seeks maximum protection for researchers, the accompanying commentary exposes the possibility or necessity for limited exceptions. Finally, the statute provides special procedures to implement the substantive objectives of the statute.

*   *   *

The proposed statute and commentary are substantially the same as submitted to the Committee on Federal Agency Evaluation Research in March, 1974. During the past summer, there have been a number of events that have considerable significance for the topics surveyed in this paper. For example, numerous cases have been decided that further define and modify the rights and obligations of journalists.[3] Litigation and prosecutions concerning the Watergate affair have continued. In particular, the U.S. Supreme Court's decision in <u>United States v. Nixon</u> affirmed a balancing test for the claim of executive privilege when in conflict with prosecutional demands.[4]

If we were to pause and attempt to assess the impact of these and other intervening developments, this paper would never be completed. However, we feel that such defects are not crucial, since this type of discussion can rarely be definitive. A central theme of the commentary to the proposed statute is that it raises confrontations of classic dimensions: e.g., the obligations of citizens to assist the state in law enforcement; the necessity for confidentiality in human relationships based on trust; and the tension between social critics and vested interests.

This complexity of issues, as well as the variety and flux of responses, has in part led us to propose a relatively absolute solution to this problem. If the reader finds the proposed statute excessive in attempting to protect the researcher-subject relationship, our defense is that we appear here as advocates of the research community. We expect that law enforcement officials, defense counsel and other advocates will continue to make their positions known. Ultimately, society--acting as judges, legislators, and administrators--will have to choose between these competing interests, either in the abstract or in specific cases. Quite probably, some limitations to the protection that we feel is necessary will prevail. But such a fundamental limitation on empirical research should not be accepted without strenuous debate.

September, 1974

SUMMARY

THE NEED FOR A STATUTE

An increasing number of behavioral and medical researchers have been confronted with compulsory process, usually by law enforcement agencies, demanding data that researchers have accumulated. Often the information demanded has been given to the researcher under an express or implied promise of confidentiality. The information is often personal and at times incriminating. To comply with the subpoenas would be harmful to the subjects and would discourage researchers from pursuing important and controversial subjects of inquiry.

Interest in protecting against abuses in the collection and dissemination of research data has been highlighted by several recent developments. The similar dilemma of protecting journalists' confidential sources and information has received wide public recognition and been the subject of frequent litigation. Researchers themselves have for the first time been subpoenaed to reveal their data, resulting in the search for new modes of protection. Increased governmental involvement in research, especially through large-scale patronage or mandatory evaluation of research programs, has led to special problems.

The prospects are slim for judicial protection of researchers, based on the First Amendment, against having to comply with compulsory process. The Supreme Court in Branzburg v. Hayes, 408 U.S. 665 (1972), rejected the assertion of a reporter's privilege based on the First Amendment. It is possible, though unlikely, that current state and proposed federal shield laws for journalists will protect researchers.

Present federal and state statutes designed to grant researchers a privilege against compulsory process are narrowly drawn, protecting only a small class of researchers. For example, the federal Comprehensive Drug Abuse Prevention Control Act of 1970 protects only those researchers "engaged in research on the use and effect of drugs."

Prosecutorial guidelines and professional codes of ethics are ineffective in protecting researchers because they are not legally enforceable. While the doctrine of executive privilege or "state and official secrets" has been suggested as a source of protection for researchers, it would only apply to immunize research data collected and stored under the auspices of governmental agencies.

A broadly drawn statute to protect the researchers and research subjects is needed.

THE NEED FOR FEDERAL LEGISLATION

While privilege conferring statutes have been traditionally legislated by the states, a federal statute would provide optimum protection. Research takes place in an interstate context and often deals with problems of national magnitude, such as drug abuse, crime control, and foreign affairs.

There is adequate constitutional basis to enact a researcher's privilege statute that would apply both on federal and state levels. The First Amendment protects the information gathering process. The authority for Congress to enact legislation that carries out policies embodied in the First Amendment is based on the positive legislative grant in section 5 of the Fourteenth Amendment. The Commerce Clause is a second constitutional basis for a federal researcher's privilege statute. It would justify protection afforded to researchers who distribute or who have some intention of distributing their information via radio, television, newspapers, journals, or books. A third basis for federal legislation is the Necessary and Proper Clause of the constitution. This would justify protection of any research done under federal auspices or research which carries out some national interest.

The proposed Statute would optimally apply equally in state and federal proceedings and would preempt all state legislation.

PERSONS COVERED

Perhaps the most difficult task in drafting this statute is defining who is a researcher. In such fields as law, medicine, or psychology, in which privileges have been established, it is a relatively easy task to extend coverage to all members of the profession. These professions have strict licensing requirments. There is no general licensing authority for researchers. The solution of licensing researchers on an ad hoc basis, used by the Comprehensive Drug Abuse Prevention and Control Act of 1970, is rejected in the Statute proposed here.

Instead, the proposed Statute attempts to protect persons involved in the research process while not immunizing every citizen from his or her duty to testify in judicial and other proceedings. Two general criteria are provided to determine whether an individual is a researcher.

First, in obtaining information, the person must employ standards or principles accepted in the field of inquiry. Specific academic methods are not necessary, nor must the individual necessarily be in an established academic field. These factors, along with past publication of research projects, academic degrees, present affiliation with a university or research center, and future intention to publish evidenced by a contract from a publisher may be relevant in establishing a bona fide involvement in research.

The second criteria is that information obtained by the researcher be gathered for the purpose of serving the general public in some foreseeable way. For example, research done solely for the internal use of a profit-making organization would not be protected by the statute. This requirement is necessary to justify federal legislation based on the First Amendment.

MATERIAL COVERED

The proposed Statute protects from compulsory process all information gathered in the course of an individual's research endeavor. This includes: (1) identity of the research subject, the most common type of information demanded; (2) contents of communications between researchers and their subjects, often closely related to subjects' identity; (3) researchers' direct observations of their subjects, a common research method; and (4) the "work product" of a researcher--notes, memoranda, unfinished manuscripts, and other records analogous to the attorney's work product.

Unlike other privilege conferring statutes, the proposed Statute does not require that there be an express or implied promise by the researcher to the subject that the information supplied be confidential.

Research subjects generally are sought after by the researcher. They rarely volunteer information conditioned on a promise of confidentiality. The subject's understanding of confidentiality is often not sophisticated. The subject presumes that the information supplied will not be turned over to the authorities. The expectation of the subject that the information supplied will not be released dictates that the statute operate regardless of whether an express or implied promise of confidentiality is made.

Furthermore, a number of traditional methodologies employed by behavioral scientists (e.g., self-description by the subject, direct observation of the subject, description of the subject by informants, and the use of other secondary data) do not provide the ideal context in which a promise for confidentiality can be made. Research subjects should not be denied protection because the research design or methodology precludes an express or implied promise of confidentiality.

SCOPE OF THE PRIVILEGE

The scope of protection granted by common law or statutory privileges has often been described as either qualified or absolute. An absolute privilege theoretically protects the beneficiaries of the privilege from compelled disclosure of specific types of information under all circumstances; a qualified privilege specifies circumstances under which the beneficiaries are not protected.

The absolute qualified dichotomy is too rigid a conceptual framework in which to consider the scope of a privilege against compelled disclosure of information. In the first place, whether a privilege is qualified or absolute is often a question of degree rather than kind. For example, a qualified privilege could protect 99 percent of all cases protected by an absolute privilege; on the other hand, it could deny protection in 99 percent of all cases. Secondly, it is difficult to imagine a privilege that is totally absolute; all privileges are subject to waiver of some type. Also, despite statutory language conferring an absolute privilege, courts may interpret the privilege to be inoperative under certain circumstances.

The proposed Statute is designed to provide maximum protection to researchers. It is divested only by waiver. The protection extends to researchers who are compelled to testify in all proceedings in which the power of compulsory process is available, including those of grand juries, legislative committees, administrative agencies, and criminal and civil courts.

The proposed Statute specifically rejects divesting the privilege in the face of a number of countervailing interests that have been exceptions to various other statutory and common law privileges. In this Statute, the privilege is not divested upon the demand of law enforcement agencies for research data. While law enforcement subpoenas have significant deterrent effects on the research process, the value of research data to law enforcement agencies is minimal. Under this Statute, the researcher is afforded protection even though the subpoena is related to national security, crimes already committed, or crimes to be committed in the future.

The proposed Statute also protects the researcher from subpoenas by defendants in criminal trials. A court may decide that the privilege couched in the First Amendment is outweighed by the Sixth Amendment right of criminal defendants to compel testimony. Because of this constitutional requirement, narrow subpoena exception for criminal defendants might be included in the statute.

The need for civil litigants to compel researchers to testify cannot be easily generalized. In comparison to criminal adjudication, however, it is rare that a civil litigant will have a constitutional interest in obtaining evidence such as that of the criminal defendant. Privilege statutes for journalists often provide for a specific exception in cases where a journalist defendant relies on an unidentified source as a defense in a libel suit. In the last decade, the U.S. Supreme Court has limited the ambit of libel actions through the landmark New York Times v. Sullivan, 376 U.S. 254 (1964), and subsequent cases. If the defendant's utterance involves a public figure, the plaintiff must sustain the heavy burden of proving that the defendant's statement was made with "actual malice"--i.e., with knowledge that it was false or with reckless disregard of whether or not it was false.

The proposed Statute rejects a libel exception to the researcher privilege in the interest of providing maximum protection. However, the rationale for the privilege is not to protect researchers from the consequences of lies that damage the reputation of their subjects. Though the likelihood of a researcher being a libel defendant is less than for a journalist, a researcher privilege statute might include a narrow exception to the privilege upon the plantiff's showing that there is a bona fide claim for defamation.

The researcher's accountability to the research community is also a concern. The research community's interest in verifying, reviewing, and analyzing data and results obtained by their fellow researchers can be met by special procedures, research designs, or extra work. No exception is made in the statute.

WAIVER

The only explicit exception to the proposed researcher's privilege is for waiver. Waiver is the power to divest the privilege by voluntarily disclosing privileged information. Most privilege conferring statutes give one party the power to waive the protection; in most professional privileges, the confider generally has the power to waive the privilege. For example, it is the patient and not the doctor, and the client and not the attorney who can waive the doctor-patient and the attorney-client privileges. A journalist's privilege, on the other hand, is generally waivable by the confidant-reporter and not the source.

The proposed Statute is unique in requiring <u>both</u> the confider-subject and the confidant-researcher to agree before the privilege is waived. The subject's interest in privacy and confidentiality as well as the researcher's interest in controlling the release of the data are both accommodated.

In cases when the researcher has obtained information from anonymous subjects, provision is made that the researcher alone can waive the privilege. This does not sacrifice the protection of research subjects, for without knowledge of the subject's identity it is difficult for the information to be used to the detriment of the subject by the subpoenaing agency.

PROCEDURES

Unlike other privilege conferring statutes, the proposed Statute's protection can be invoked by any person having knowledge of research data. That person need not be a researcher or a research subject.

The burden of proving that the Statute applies to an individual rests upon the individual asserting the privilege. Because the statute protects a wide class, it should not be a difficult burden for a bona fide researcher to sustain.

The most important procedural provisions of the proposed Statute are the requirements that must be met before a subpoena can be issued. The issuer must sustain a heavy factual burden of need for the information before a subpoena will even be issued to a researcher. This will prevent harassment of researchers by subpoena-issuing agencies and will enhance the substantive protection granted by the statute.

AN ACT TO PROTECT RESEARCHERS
AND THEIR SUBJECTS

Section 1: Purposes
   The purposes of this Act include the following:
      (1) to enhance the flow of information to the public;
      (2) to allow the researcher to investigate controversial areas with minimum interference; and
      (3) to allow research subjects to be candid in their responses without fear of having the information used to their detriment.

Section 2: Creation of a Privilege for Researchers
   No person shall be compelled pursuant to a subpoena or other legal process issued under the authority of the United States or any State during the course of any judicial, administrative, or legislative investigation or adjudicative proceeding to give testimony or to produce any information storing device, object, or thing that would--
      (1) reveal any subject or impair any subject relationship by revealing the identity of the subject or the contents of information received, observed, developed, or maintained by a researcher, whether or not any explicit or implicit promise of confidentiality had been made to the subject, in the course of gathering, compiling, storing, analyzing, reviewing, editing, disseminating by any media, or publishing any research data, or
      (2) reveal the contents of any information received, developed, or maintained by a researcher in the course of gathering, compiling, storing, analyzing, composing, reviewing, editing, disseminating by any media, or publishing any research data.

Section 3: Waiver
   (a) The privilege conferred in section 2 of this Act is waived only when--
      (1) the researcher is compelled to disclose information pursuant to a subpoena or other legal process and both the researcher and subject knowingly and voluntarily consent to a waiver.
         (A) The researcher must sustain the burden of proving the subject's consent, either by producing a written statement signed by the subject or his agent or by the subject personally appearing before the body issuing the subpoena or other legal process.
         (B) When the researcher does not have knowledge of the identity of the subject, the requirement of subsection 1 (A) of this section need not be met.

(2) The subject is compelled to disclose information pursuant to a subpoena or other legal process and the subject knowingly and voluntarily consents to a waiver.

(b) The disclosure of information by a researcher or subject pursuant to this section shall not constitute a waiver for that part of the information not disclosed.

Section 4: Presubpoena Standards

(a) No subpoena or other legal process to compel the testimony of a researcher or the production of any information storing device, object, or thing shall be issued under the authority of the United States or any State except upon a finding that--

(1) there are reasonable grounds to believe that the researcher has information which is (A) not within the privilege set forth in section 2 of the Act, and (B) material to a particular investigation or controversy within the jurisdiction of the issuing body or person;

(2) there is a factual basis for the investigation or for the claim of the party to the controversy to which the researcher's information relates; and

(3) the same or equivalent information is not available to the issuing person or body from any source other than a researcher.

(b) A finding pursuant to subsection (a) of this section shall be made--

(1) in the case of a court, grand jury, or any officer empowered to institute or bind over upon criminal charges by a judge of the court;

(2) in the case of a legislative body, committee, or subcommittee, by the cognizant body, committee, or subcommittee;

(3) in the case of an executive department or agency, by the chief officer of the department or agency; and

(4) in the case of an independent commission, board, or agency, by the commission, board, or agency.

(c) A finding pursuant to subsection (a) of this section shall be made on the record after hearing. Adequate notice of the hearing and opportunity to be heard shall be given to the researcher.

(d) An order of a court issuing or refusing to issue a subpoena or other legal process pursuant to subsection (a) of this section shall be an appealable order and shall be stayed by the court for a reasonable time to permit appellate review.

(e) A finding pursuant to subsection (a) of this section made by a body, agency, or other entity described in clause (2), (3), or (4) of subsection (b) of this section shall be subject to judicial review, and the issuance of the subpoena or other legal process shall be stayed by the issuing body, agency, or other entity for a reasonable time to permit judicial review.

Section 5: Definitions

For the purposes of this Act:

(1) The term "researcher" means any individual who is or was at the time of exposure to the information or thing sought by subpoena or other legal process engaged in gathering, compiling, storing, analyzing, reviewing, editing, disseminating through any media, or publishing research data.

(2) The term "research data" means any information obtained by employing standards accepted in the field of inquiry and for the purpose of public benefit.

(3) The term "information storing device" means any paper, recording, film, microfilm, microfiche, tape, card, print-out, or any other device by which information is stored.

(4) The term "media" means any periodical, journal, book, report, study, thesis, radio or television broadcast, cable television transmission, or other means, published or unpublished, by which research data is reported.

(5) The term "subject" means any individual whose actions or responses are being studied by a researcher.

COMMENTARY

THE NEED FOR STATUTORY PROTECTION

Recent Demands for Research Data

Two ways of judging the need for protection are published case histories of individual experiences and more general surveys of the research community.

Case Histories

The variety of the cases to date emphasizes the need for broad protection. For instance, requests were made not only by prosecutors but also by legislative committees and defense counsel. In some cases, the researcher was operating in a traditional academic setting; in others, the researcher was a freelance author or the member of a public commission. Funding sources included federal and state governments, as well as private foundations.

All of the research mentioned had the purpose of expanding knowledge and informing the public, but it also had a variety of other goals: some researchers were evaluating federal programs; some were examining topical issues, such as the Vietnam war or Attica; some were engaged in experimentation, such as drug abuse prevention and control; and some were conducting basic research.

In the early 1950's, the Kinsey Institute conducted a controversial study of sexual practices in the United States. Both the FBI and the U.S. State Department requested information about individuals who had allegedly participated in the study.[5] The Institute was deeply concerned with maintaining the confidence of its subjects. It stated that, in the absence of judicial recognition of a privilege between the researcher and his subject, the information would be destroyed and the Institute would accept the consequences.[6] The federal government, upon the Institute's refusal to produce the records, did not press its demands.

The Institute for Research on Poverty at the University of Wisconsin and Mathematica, a private New Jersey organization, were funded by the U.S. Office of Economic Opportunity (OEO) to evaluate the New Jersey negative income tax experiment.[7] The research involved interviewing all participants in the experiment and eliciting information as to the families' earnings, hours worked, attitudes toward work, family stability, and other indicia of social and psychological behavior. The information was obtained under an explicit pledge of confidentiality. The case records compiled by the researchers were subpoenaed by the local county prosecutor investigating whether families were receiving welfare payments under the New Jersey welfare program in addition to the aid received under the federal experiment. Extensive negotiations between the prosecutor and the researchers resulted in an agreement not to subpoena the records in return for the researchers' cooperation in comparing the families participating in the federal program with those on the New Jersey welfare rolls, and OEO reimbursed the state agency. The research on the effect of the negative income tax experiment was, nevertheless, jeopardized by the prosecutor's action. Subsequently, the Finance Committee of the U.S. Senate requested the researchers to produce the files of six participating families so that it could verify OEO's preliminary report. The researchers refused the request, and the demand was finally dropped.

In another case, the American Council on Education (ACE) conducted a longitudinal study on campus unrest and violence. Sensitive data were collected on individual subjects.[8] The National Student Association and Students for a Democratic Society feared that the data would get into the "wrong hands." These fears were borne out when several governmental agencies made known their plans to subpoena the records. The ACE response was to draw up guidelines relating to the confidentiality of the data it received. This case highlights the potentiality for the researcher to be converted into an arm of the government at a moment's notice.

The government investigation of the release of the "Pentagon Papers" led to the subpoenaing of a large number of scholars involved in the study of U.S. foreign policy and Vietnamese life.

Samuel Popkin, an assistant professor of government at Harvard University, was subpoenaed by the federal grand jury investigating the release of the "Pentagon Papers."[9] In an appearance before the grand jury, Popkin was questioned on information he obtained while doing research in the United States and Vietnam. He refused to answer questions relating to conversations with confidential sources about who participated in preparing the "Pentagon Papers." He also refused to state whether he had spoken to Daniel Ellsberg about the existence of the "Pentagon Papers" and to reveal persons he believed possessed the "Papers" before their publication in The Washington Post and The New York Times. Popkin was jailed for contempt of court based on these refusals. He was released when the grand jury investigating the case was dismissed. Though upholding the contempt charge and deciding against a researcher's privilege on the facts of the case,[10] the U.S. First Circuit Court of Appeals aptly identified the issue at stake as follows:

> [A researcher's] privilege, if it exists, exists because an important public interest in the continued flow of information to scholars about public problems would stop if scholars could be forced to disclose the sources of such information. As is true of other behavior scientists, his research technique rests heavily on inquiry of others as to their attitudes, knowledge or experience. Often such inquiry is predicated on a relationship of confidence.[11]

The U.S. Supreme Court refused to hear Popkin's appeal.

Richard Falk, a professor of international relations at Princeton University, was similarly subpoenaed by the federal grand jury in Massachusetts.[12] In his motion to quash the subpoena, Falk argued that a "mere appearance" before the grand jury would impair the effectiveness of his professional involvement in writing and advising on the American role in the Vietnam war; he would lose the confidence of individuals upon whom he depended for information and would not be given further access to confidential material. In denying his motion to quash, the district court stated that there was "no real likelihood" that Falk's sources would be inhibited by his grand jury appearance.

The Massachusetts federal grand jury also subpoenaed Leonard S. Rodberg, a resident fellow at the Institute for Policy Studies. Rodberg had joined the staff of Senator Mike Gravel on the day that Gravel placed the "Pentagon Papers" in the public record, making them available for publication by the press. Rodberg, in his motion to quash the subpoena, argued that his appearance before the grand jury would jeopardize his ability as a researcher to communicate his findings to the public and to advise the Congress on government policy.[13] This agreement was rejected by the district court and not considered by the U.S. Court of Appeals or the U.S. Supreme Court.

With Senator Gravel as intervenor, Rodberg further argued that the subpoena violated the Speech and Debate Clause of the U.S. Constitution, conferring a congressional privilege.[14] The U.S. Supreme Court[15] ultimately decided that, while the congressional privilege did apply to the aides of members of Congress, it did not immunize Rodberg from complying with a subpoena requesting information relating to the private publication of the "Pentagon Papers," which was viewed to have no connection with the legislative process.

A commission was appointed by Governor Rockefeller of New York to investigate the riot and deaths that occurred at the Attica prison in September 1971. After interviewing thousands of witnesses under a pledge of confidentiality and publishing the report, the commission was subpoenaed by the attorney general's office to produce all its records. The attorney general was in the process of conducting his own investigation of the Attica situation relating to the issue of possible criminal liability. The New York State Supreme Court ruled that the information collected by the commission was immune from the attorney general's subpoena on the basis of "public interest" privilege.[16]

In a final example, a witness to a murder in New York City told police that she believed that she had seen the killer in the waiting room of a methadone clinic. A subpoena was subsequently served on Dr. Robert Newman, director of the methadone program in question, requiring that they photograph all males between the ages of 21 and 35 who were patients at the clinic to which the witness referred.[17] Dr. Newman's motion to quash the subpoena in the New York Supreme Court, based on a federal statute and the state doctor-patient privilege, was rejected. He was held in contempt of court and sentenced to 30 days in jail. The appellate division of the New York Supreme Court upheld the contempt order. A subsequent appeal was taken by Dr. Newman to the New York Court of Appeals which overruled the contempt order. The Court held that the photographs were privileged under the confidentiality provisions of the Federal Drug Abuse Prevention and Control Act of 1970, protecting information obtained in the course of drug research.

These case histories, combined with the even more celebrated litigation involving reporters, have inspired increased consciousness on the part of individuals and groups of researchers to devise means by which to protect researchers from compulsory disclosure of data. The effect of the Popkin litigation has been the most conspicuous. Several professional associations, including the American Political Science Association, banded together as amicus curiae in filing a brief in support of Popkin's petition for certiorari to the U.S. Supreme Court. The Council of the American Sociological Association, representing 15,000 members, adopted the following broad resolution at its San Francisco meeting in December, 1972:

> Whereas the ASA deplores the recent imprisonment of Professor Samuel Popkin of Harvard University, who was held in civil contempt of federal grand jury for refusing to disclose the names of persons with whom he had discussed the secret war study carried out by the Pentagon; and
> Whereas we conclude that the Department of Justice, both pressing the case and imposing the sanctions of imprisonment, has taken a serious and oppressive step in chilling free scholarly inquiry; therefore be it
> Resolved, that we, as a professional association of social scientists, urge that our colleagues and the general public be aware of and take action appropriate to prevent the recurrence of such arbitrary and oppressive use of prosecutorial and judicial power against scholars.[18]

Surveys of the Research Community

These case histories highlight the need for a researcher's shield law. An empirical study of the unreported experiences of researchers in the United States would, however, probably make the case for a shield law stronger. Two surveys already undertaken point out the character of responses that may be obtained by such a study and can serve as models.

The Study Report for the Reporter's Committee for Freedom of the Press prepared by Professor Vince Blasi of the University of Michigan Law School, Press Subpoenas: An Empirical and Legal Analysis, surveyed reporters throughout the United States. Employing personal interviews and essay-type, short-answer questionnaires, Blasi defined the magnitude and scope of the problem that the press was experiencing because of the use or threat of the use of the power to compel testimony possessed by numerous arms of government. Slightly more than half of the 975 reporters surveyed relied on confidential sources in more than ten percent of their articles.[19] Eight percent of this group stated with certainty that the press subpoena threat adversely affected their relationships with confidential sources, and 11 percent were unsure if they were adversely affected.[20] Blasi also explored the desires of reporters in terms of the type of shield law that should be enacted.

Dr. Albin Eser, a law professor in West Germany, has conducted an empirical study of the problems encountered by researchers in his country in obtaining and protecting information from confidential sources.[21] Dr. Eser surveyed 218 researchers, primarily (but not limited to) individuals studying criminal law and criminology in West Germany. The preliminary results of the survey reveal that 18 percent or 26 of the 146 respondents encountered some problem with public authorities, such as the police or prosecutor, either in obtaining information or withholding confidential data. In addition to the 26 who reported problems, a number of other researchers stated that they had experienced problems but did not want to reveal them for fear of repercussion by the authorities.

Current Judicial Protection

Absent a statute that protects the researcher from compelled disclosure of information, the prospects for effective judicial protection under the First Amendment are poor. The ruling of the United States Supreme Court in Branzburg v. Hayes,[22] failing by a 5-4 vote to find a testimonial privilege based on the First Amendment for reporters appearing before a grand jury, reflects both the reluctance of the judiciary to provide writers with adequate protection and the need for legislation. Branzburg, however, did allow for some judicial protection of journalists based on the First Amendment. Lower federal courts have subsequently attempted to grant journalists First Amendment protection against compelled testimony while remaining consistent with Branzburg.

In discussing the meaning of the word "press" in the First Amendment, the Court in Branzburg noted:

> Freedom of press . . . is not confined to newspapers and periodicals . . . [but includes] pamphlets and leaflets [and] comprehends every sort of publication which affords a vehicle of information and opinion.[23]

The Court continued:

> The information function assured by representatives of the organized press in the present cases is also performed by lecturers, political pollsters, novelists, academic researchers and dramatists [emphasis added].[24]

Similarly, one commentator aptly described the researcher as "a slow journalist."[25]

Substantively, the greatest blow to the judicial establishment of a testimonial privilege for journalists, and thus by analogy for researchers, was the U.S. Supreme Court's refusal in Branzburg to "grant newsmen a first amendment testimonial privilege [before a grand jury in a criminal case] that other citizens do not enjoy."[26] Referring to the records documenting the importance of a confidential journalist-source relationship presented to the Court by the various petitioners, Justice White, speaking for the majority, stated:

> We perceive no basis for holding that the public interest in law enforcement and insuring effective grand jury proceedings is insufficient to override the consequential, but uncertain, burden of newsgathering that is said to result from insisting that reporters like other citizens respond to relevant questions put to them in the course of a valid grand jury investigation or criminal trial.[27]

The Branzburg Court, however, did qualify to some extent what at first blush seemed to be the total rejection of a reporter's privilege. In the first place, the Court emphasized the importance of the grand jury's role in investigating crime, thereby "securing the safety of the person and property of the citizen."[28] The governmental interest furthered by the grand jury was sufficient, in the Court's opinion, to meet the requirement that even indirect burdens upon the First Amendment rights be justified by a "paramount" or "compelling" state interest. The U.S. Supreme Court thus suggested that in certain contexts the First Amendment infringement may not be sufficiently justified.

Since Branzburg, lower federal courts, in accordance with this suggestion, have distinguished between civil and criminal cases. It is more likely for the reporters to be granted the privilege in civil than in criminal cases.

Baker v. F & F Investment,[29] for example, involved a civil rights class action brought by a group of blacks in Chicago challenging the racially discriminatory block-busting practices and inflated prices that were employed by real estate agencies. A reporter, Alfred Balk, was deposed by the plaintiffs because he had written a magazine article about the experiences of an anonymous real estate agent in Chicago. While sympathetic to the plaintiffs, Balk refused to divulge the name of the subject of the article because this was given to him on a confidential basis. The court denied the plaintiffs' motion to compel disclosure under Rule 37 of the Federal Rules of Criminal Procedure, largely because this was a civil case, in contrast to the criminal investigation in Branzburg. In the context of this case, the court found no compelling reason to override the First Amendment.

Similarly, a federal district court held for reporters in Democratic National Committee v. McCord,[30] emphasizing that this was a civil action. Subpoenas were served upon reporters and management personnel of The New York Times, the Washington Post, Time, and the Washington Star-News on behalf of the Committee for the Re-election of the President and the Finance Committee to Re-elect the President and its chairman, all of whom were parties to the civil action pertaining to the break-in at Democratic National Headquarters at Watergate. The subpoenas called for the production of all documents, papers, and photos relating to the Watergate incident. Ten motions to quash these subpoenas were granted the reporters and newspaper management personnel in a decision stating that the movants were entitled to a qualified privilege from compelled disclosure under the facts of the cases presented.[31]

In contrast to McCord, reporters in United States v. Liddy[32] were denied motions to quash defense subpoenas issued during a criminal trial involving the Watergate burglary and bugging. Though Branzburg dealt specifically with a grand jury, the court believed that the principles there enunciated could pertain equally in the criminal trial.

A second qualification in the Branzburg decision is the Court's explicit recognition of the general First Amendment limitations placed on all investigative proceedings.[33] While in the federal system the grand jury's investigative power has been held to be necessarily broad,[34] the grand jury cannot ask questions that have no relation to the purpose of its investigation.[35] Nor can grand juries require witnesses to reveal the names of organizations and their members that have no relation to the crime being investigated.[36] Furthermore, with specific relevance to reporters, the Court stated that "official harassment of the press undertaken not for purposes of law enforcement but to disrupt a reporter's relationship with his news source would have no justification."[37]

The final qualification to the Branzburg decision is the short yet potentially potent concurrence by Justice Powell, who joined with Chief Justice

Burger and Justices White, Rehnquist, and Blackman to form the Branzburg majority. The thrust of the concurrence is Powell's belief that

> the asserted claim to a privilege should be judged on the facts of each case by striking a balance between freedom of the press and the obligation of all citizens to give relevant testimony with respect to criminal conduct.[38]

It is, therefore, possible that upon a different set of facts Justice Powell would join the minority in Branzburg,[39] holding in favor of a reporter's privilege. Lower federal courts have, in fact, utilized Justice Powell's balancing approach when presented with a reporter's claim of privilege.[40]

The Branzburg decision, thus, does not totally rule out the First Amendment as a potential source of some protection for newsmen and researchers. This protection, however, is inadequate to assure researchers that they will be able to pursue their work without impediment. The only definite assurance is that courts will quash subpoenas that are designed to harass and that deliberately impair the relationship between the researcher and the subject. This, however, is likely to be a rare occurence and difficult for the researcher to prove.

In criminal cases, the public interest in law enforcement served by prosecutorial subpoenas and the individual's Sixth Amendment interests in confrontation and compulsory process served by defendant's subpoenas will generally be sufficient to override the researcher's First Amendment interest.

In civil cases, a court is more apt to objectively consider the competing interests on both sides. The First Amendment interest of the researcher will generally be outweighed only when the individual issuing the subpoena or other legal process shows a specific purpose for the information and shows that it cannot be obtained from an alternate source. There is, however, no way in which a researcher can predict whether or not the court will decide that the interests in compelled disclosure outweigh the First Amendment interest in informing the public through research. Without assurance that certain material will be immune from compulsory disclosure, the researcher will necessarily be inhibited.

Post-Branzburg Press Subpoenas

The Report of the American Bar Association Study Group on Journalist's Shield Legislation contains the following compilation of instances in which reporters have been imprisoned or threatened with imprisonment within six months after the Supreme Court's Branzburg decision. These case histories graphically point out that journalists and, thus, researchers are in need of protection beyond judicial application of the First Amendment if they are to be able to effectively resist subpoenas or other legal process that infringe upon their relationships with human subjects.

1. On July 7, 1972, Peter Bridge,[41] a reporter in Newark, New Jersey, was held in contempt for refusing to disclose unpublished information on local corruption before a grand jury. The order was affirmed by the New Jersey appellate courts. Bridge was jailed on October 3, 1972, and spent 21 days in custody. His incarceration prevented his appearance before the House Judiciary Subcommittee considering protection of news sources, but Bridge submitted a statement to the House Subcommittee in which he said, inter alia:

B-19

>   As a reporter with 13 years in the profession, I can
>   testify that confidential sources comprise the single
>   most important device in the effective gathering of
>   information. Any threat to the use of that device
>   threatens the destruction of a free press.[42]

2. On October 17, 1972, the Maryland Court of Appeals affirmed the contempt citation of a Baltimore reporter, David Lightman.[43] Lightman was held in contempt for declining to disclose his sources of information relating to drug abuse by youthful users at a Maryland resort.

3. On September 11, 1972, a committee of the Tennessee State Senate issued an order against a Memphis newsman, Joseph Weiler, directing him to show cause why he should not be held in contempt of the legislature for declining to disclose the sources of his information as to child abuse at a hospital and school for retarded children. The contempt hearing was cancelled only when the Tennessee attorney general ruled that the committee lacked the authority to conduct it.[44] A Memphis radio newsman, Joseph Pennington, who reported on the same matters, was compelled by the contempt threats of this committee to disclose the sources of his story.[45]

4. On October 11, 1972, three reporters in Milwaukee, Gene Cunningham, Dean Jensen, and Stuart Wilk, were ordered to disclose confidential sources of information relating to alleged improprieties of a county official.[46]

5. On December 19, 1972, a grand jury subpoena was issued for James Mitchell, a Los Angeles radio news reporter, to require him to produce tapes of interviews he conducted during an investigation of corrupt bail bond practices. The subpoena was later quashed by the Los Angeles County District Attorney's Office.[47]

6. On November 28, 1972, Harry Thornton, a newsman for a television station in Chattanooga, Tennessee, was held in contempt for declining to disclose the confidential source of information relating to the grand jury investigation of a local judge. He was jailed briefly until a stay was granted by an appellate court.[48]

7. On December 19, 1972, John F. Lawrence, a _Los Angeles Times_ newsman, was held in contempt in a proceeding in the U.S. District Court in Washington, D.C., for declining to turn over certain tape recordings of interviews and other unpublished information gathered by reporters of the _Times_. He was briefly imprisoned, until a stay was granted by an appellate court.[49]

8. Other representatives of the news media have testified before Congress that they have been unable to conduct interviews with news sources because of inability to assure the sources of confidentiality.[50]

These examples of impairment of the freedom to gather the news could be multiplied. The list is illustrative, not exhaustive, of the spread of restraints on the free flow of information.

Statutes: Existing and Proposed

The necessity of protecting the researcher from compulsory disclosure of information is underscored by both existing statutes designed to protect particular types of research activity and by proposed federal and existing state privilege laws for journalists that might protect certain types of researchers.

This section will focus on the threshold concern of the coverage of existing and proposed legislation.[51] In the absence of specific statutory protection for researchers in general, a continuing question is whether existing and proposed laws will cover a broad or narrow group of individuals engaged in research.

Present Statutes Concerning Research

There are only a handful of federal and state statutes that are specifically designed to protect researchers or research activity. These statutes provide protection for only a small minority of individuals.

Both Maryland and New York have statutes that protect specific data associated with specific research projects. The New York statute[52] pertains only to the multistate information system for psychiatric patients. This is a research and demonstration project designed to study the possibility of improving medical information through the use of computer-based systems and aggregate statistics in planning and operating psychiatric hospitals. Within the project the statute immunizes from the subpoena power of any court or administrative agency only the records and information pertaining to patients outside of New York State.

The Maryland law[53] makes inadmissible "records, reports, statements, notes, or other information . . . assembled or procured by the State Board of Health and Mental Hygiene or . . . for the Maryland Commission to Study Problems of Drug Addiction . . ." The statute also immunizes agents of the Commission and the Board from being compelled to disclose this information. The data attains privileged status only if it is procured for the purposes specified in the statutes defining the Board and Commission.[54] Few researchers can expect protection under such narrowly drawn statutes, which protect only specific data compiled by specified agencies.

The U.S. Congress has passed a series of statutes that protect a wider class of researchers than the state statutes mentioned. At best, though, these federal statutes still cover only a relatively small group of researchers. Pursuant to the Comprehensive Drug Abuse Prevention and Control Act of 1970,[55] the Secretary of Health, Education, and Welfare[56] and the U.S. Attorney General[57] may grant a testimonial privilege to persons "engaged in research on the use and effect of drugs." These provisions focus on a particular type of research rather than specific data compiled in the courts of a stated research project.

The legislative history of the Drug Abuse provisions indicates that the privilege can be granted both to federally funded and non-federally funded drug researchers.[58] The statute's coverage at most, therefore, extends only to all persons involved in drug research. The coverage of the statute is further limited by the necessity of specifically applying to the Secretary of Health, Education, and Welfare or the U.S. Attorney General for a grant of confidentially.[59] An administrative procedure has been devised by which the Secretary of Health, Education, and Welfare, through the National Institute of Mental Health, must approve the bona fides of the drug research project, and the U.S. Attorney General, through the Bureau of Narcotics and Dangerous Drugs, must approve the security precautions taken by the researchers in handling the drug.[60] The coverage of these provisions is, thus, limited by the statutory discretion granted to the Secretary of Health, Education, and Welfare and the U.S. Attorney General, as well as by the administrative procedures devised.

An analogous provision to that granting discretion to the Secretary of Health, Education, and Welfare to provide drug researchers with a privilege is included in the Comprehensive Alcohol and Alcoholism Prevention, Treatment, and Rehabilitation Act of 1970.[61] The Secretary may grant a privilege to "persons engaged in research in or treatment with respect to alcohol abuse and alcoholism."[62] The coverage of this provision is also limited to a specific class of researchers and is subject to the discretion of the Secretary of Health, Education, and Welfare.

A major drawback of the confidentiality provisions of the Drug Abuse Act and the Alcoholism Act is that they condition protection on the discretion of the Secretary of Health, Education, and Welfare or the U.S. Attorney General. Such discretion, as well as the requirement that researchers be "licensed" before they receive protection, could severely threaten the freedom of researchers to pursue controversial avenues of inquiry. Those with the power to grant protection to researchers or to license them could potentially abuse this power to control the type of research pursued. Any researchers who, for example, did not threaten to criticize the government or to undermine established theories would be given protection, while other researchers would have to risk being compelled to reveal information.

A more limited, yet complementary, provision[63] to the confidentiality granted by the Drug Abuse Prevention and Control Act of 1970 is the grant of confidentiality conferred by the Drug Abuse Office and Treatment Act of 1972.[64] It confers a qualified privilege to "records of the identity, diagnosis, prognosis, or treatment of any patient which are maintained in connection with the performance of any drug abuse prevention function . . ."[65] Drug abuse prevention function specifically includes research.[66] Unlike the New York and Maryland statutes, the 1972 drug abuse prevention provision does not apply only to specific projects or agencies; like the state laws, the privilege is granted only to data maintained by researchers involved in a particular type of research, that on drugs.

Further privileges[67] created by Congress, while not specifically designed to protect researchers or data obtained in the courts of research, may provide some protection within the researcher-subject context. The provisions prohibiting disclosure of census information and creating a privileged status for retained copies of census reports[68] protect social science research undertaken by the government and mandated by the Constitution.[69] Also protected from disclosure by federal statute are records of the U.S. Social Security Administration,[70] which also contain data similar to that elicited by social scientists in the private sector. The protection granted by these statutes extends, however, to the limited group of researchers who work for the U.S. Census Bureau or Social Security Administration.

Relevant Statutes for Journalists

A number of existing state privilege statutes for journalists, as well as a number of privilege bills now before Congress in the wake of Branzburg v. Hayes,[71] potentially afford protection to a wider class of researchers than state and federal statutes specifically designed to protect researchers. A number of statutes[72] and proposals[73] are narrowly drawn, extending coverage, for example, only to regularly employed reporters of newspapers at a specific circulation. Such statutes clearly do not cover researchers.

The applicability of broad newsman statutes to the researcher stems from the overlap between the functions the researcher and the journalist serve in society. One observer aptly described a researcher as a "slow journalist." Testifying before Congress, Richard Barnet, author and political scientist, pointed out that modern society is too complex to leave the task of keeping the public informed to the journalist. Investigations by scholars in the form of books, pamphlets, television reports, mimeographs, and studies fill the gaps where journalists cannot perform effectively. And Justice White, speaking for the majority in <u>Branzburg</u>, pointed to the conceptual similarity between journalists and researchers when he stated that:

> The information function asserted by representatives of the organized press . . . is also performed by lecturers, political pollsters, novelists, academic researchers and dramatists.[75]

In examining the specific language of broadly drawn statutes and bills, it becomes apparent that these measures do not sufficiently cover researchers in general to obviate the need for a specific statute designed to protect the research community.[76]

The state shield laws currently in effect in Alaska, Arkansas, and Minnesota arguably cover researchers. The Alaska statute[77] applies to any "public official or reporter . . . while acting in the course of his duties as a public official or reporter." The terms "public official" and "reporter" are left undefined by the statute, thus, leaving it generally up to the courts to decide if an individual is covered. Though the interpretation is doubtful, the term "public official" could conceivably embrace any individual funded by the government, thereby potentially covering any researcher supported by government funds. More likely, however, the term refers to individuals who hold a specific public office, such as mayor, governor, legislator, or school board president. The term "reporter" is similarly ambiguous. A broad interpretation would include any individual who disseminates information through any media, including radio, television, newspapers of all types, magazines, books, and films. A narrow and more conventional interpretation would restrict the term "reporter" to individuals who write stories for newspapers and magazines. Despite the possibilities for broad interpretation to include researchers of some types, the Alaska statute provides no assurance that a researcher will be afforded protection. The statute, therefore, is highly unsatisfactory to individuals engaged in controversial research whose projects depend upon confidentiality.

The Arkansas statute[78] is less ambiguous than that of Alaska but also less inclusive. It protects "any editor, reporter or other writer for any newspaper or periodical or manager or owner of any radio station." In its broadest interpretation, this statute, which requires some type of affiliation with a newspaper, magazine or radio station, would exclude many individuals involved in research. For example, the large class of researchers working in universities or for governmental agencies generally remain unprotected. Furthermore, while many researchers will at some point in their career publish a journal article, thereby affiliating with a periodical, the statute appears to cover only research that is so reported. Finally, the statute excludes important types of media associated with researchers, most obviously books, tapes, and films. The Arkansas shield law, thus, does not assure a sufficiently wide spectrum of researchers the protection they need.

The Minnesota Free Flow of Information Act is a recently enacted "newsman" shield law.[79] Of all the statutes that have actually been enacted, the Minnesota law provides for the widest coverage. Any "person who is or has been directly engaged in the gathering, procuring, compiling, editing, or publishing of information for purpose of transmission, dissemination or publication to the public"[80] is protected. On its face, the Minnesota statute extends protection to all individuals who have access to information; the only qualification is that the information be utilized "for the purpose of transmitting or disseminating it to the public." It would, therefore, protect a large number of researchers as researchers often have as an identifiable aim the dissemination in some form of the information with which they deal. The phrase "for the purpose of," however, may be interpreted as requiring that dissemination or transmittal be the proximate goal of the person dealing with the information. Many researchers may be found to have some other proximate goal, such as evaluating a particular governmental program or curing a disease. Dissemination or transmittal to the public would, thus, be viewed as a more remote, ultimate goal and render many researchers unprotected. Even a statute as broad as Minnesota's potentially leaves many individuals involved in research unprotected.

It is useful to examine the applicability to researchers of broad journalists' shield laws currently being considered by the U.S. Congress. The language of many of these bills arguably covers some researchers. The intention of Congress as reflected in its reports and elicited testimony, however, focuses on traditional news media. Rarely were the specific needs of the research community considered.

One bill that provides wide coverage is that proposed by Congressman Reid.[81] It extends protection to "journalists"[82] and any "news media."[83] The definition of "journalist" potentially limits coverage to only certain individuals engaged in research. While "journalist" includes people handling information for books, many researchers communicate their findings in unpublished monographs and lectures to colleagues. Such individuals would probably be excluded from statutory protection. Furthermore, the term "journalist" itself is specifically associated with the news media and not with researchers. A court is likely to confine the statute's protection to those who traditionally fit within this general connotation of the term "journalist."

Another broad bill presently before Congress is that presented by Senator Cranston.[84] It protects individuals handling information "for any medium of communication to the public." The language of this bill would arguably protect a wide class of researchers. The terms used in the bill such as "news," "edit," "wire service," "broadcast station"--while not precluding protection of researchers--focus the coverage of the bill specifically towards individuals associated with the news media. A court may, thus, so limit the protection of the bill.

Other Possible Solutions

Researchers can be protected from compelled disclosure of information in a number of ways. No solution to the problem of immunizing researchers from compulsory process[85] so that they may investigate important and controversial areas provides as potentially broad and reliable protection as legislation. This section will survey the inadequacies of some of the non-constitutional, non-statutory strategies for establishing a privilege for researchers.

Professional Codes

One possible source of protection from compulsory process is professional codes of ethics, which provide a model of behavior for researchers who are members of established professional societies.[86] Many of these codes of ethics include specific provisions on confidentiality.[87] A court may be reluctant to disregard a professional code of ethics when confronted with a situation in which a researcher is attaching a subpoena. On the basis of the professional code, the court might uphold the researcher's motion to quash the subpoena.

Researchers, however, can in no way rely on a court's adherence to the confidentiality provision of the ethical code promulgated by their profession. This was pointed out in the journalist's area where, despite a strong professional ethic against disclosure of confidential information,[88] the Supreme Court in Branzburg made it difficult for the judiciary throughout the country to hold in favor of a common law journalist's privilege. The applicability of professional codes in the establishment of a researcher's privilege is further limited by the fact that some researchers are not tied to the professional organization that promulgate codes of ethics.

Project Guidelines

A second method by which researchers can help protect themselves from compelled disclosure of information is to provide project guidelines obligating researchers to maintain confidentiality and stating that the sponsor will support the researcher if a subpoena is served. This tack was taken by the research advisory committee for the American Council on Education (ACE) campus unrest study. The guidelines provided that:

> 5. [The researcher involved in the project] will explicitly undertake to protect all confidential information, whether recorded or not, that is revealed to them. They will specifically agree to refuse to divulge confidential information to any group including investigative agencies, committees, and courts of law, and even if they or their records should be subpoenaed.
> 6. . . . [The committee] advise and counsel all researchers in their study to refuse to release or provide any confidential information, even if directed to do so by subpoena or other court proceedings from a legislative body or court of law. We will support with all legal means any such refusals.[89]

Project guidelines potentially provide better protection than professional codes of ethics because they focus upon a single research project, specifically obligating researchers involved to maintain confidentiality. In stating that the project sponsors will support the researcher's refusal to divulge, the researcher at least is provided with the financial resources and possibly benefited by the reputation of the sponsor in litigation that may arise.

Despite their advantages over codes of ethics, however, project guidelines have weaknesses similar to those of professional codes. They may be persuasive to a court of law in deciding in favor of a researcher's privilege, but they are in no way legally binding. Furthermore, they can only protect researchers affiliated with sponsoring organizations. Freelancers and researchers involved in research independent of a large-scale project remain without protection.

Executive Privilege

It has been suggested in one source[90] that the doctrine of executive privilege or "state and official secrets"[91] be extended to protect the confidentiality of research data collected by individuals engaged in governmental research. On the federal level, for example, agencies are generally empowered under the "housekeeping statute"[92] to promulgate regulations to promote efficient administration. Under this authority, the administrators of the federal agencies can "regulate the usage of records and information" belonging to that agency. The administrator, in effect, could thus claim a privilege for agency records if subpoenaed."[93]

Executive privilege as a means of protecting researchers from compulsory disclosure of information has been criticized by the authority suggesting it[94] as well as by other legal scholars.[95] In the first place, it applies only to government research; research activity in general could thus not be protected. Also, executive privilege could apply only to records physically retained by the particular state or federal agency. Finally, such laws as the federal housekeeping statute caution against withholding information from the public. Coupled with the policy of the Freedom of Information Act,[96] courts may be reluctant to confer a privilege against compulsory disclosure of research data based in regulations promulgated by federal agencies.

Prosecutorial Guidelines

A further means of protecting the confidentiality of research data is for law enforcement agencies to promulgate guidelines that specify standards for subpoenaing researchers similar to those issued by the U.S. Department of Justice regarding the news media.[97] The prosecutorial gudelines would recognize that there is an important social interest in restricting the use of researcher subpoenas. They would state that the researcher is not an investigative arm of the government and would specify limited situations in which the need of law enforcement agencies outweighs the interest in immunizing researchers from the subpoena power. Finally, the guidelines would require that the law enforcement agency and the researchers negotiate before a subpoena, which could only be issued by the agency's chief officer, is served.[98]

While prosecutorial guidelines are a good first step in providing researchers with protection against compulsory disclosure of information, they are not wholly satisfactory. Empirically, the Department of Justice's Press Subpoena Guidelines, although lauded by Branzburg,[99] have not curtailed press subpoenas to a large extent,[100] particularly at the state level. Furthermore, the guidelines apply only to prosecutors; they do not extend to other agencies that possess the power to compel testimony, such as legislative and administrative hearings, nor do they apply to criminal defendants or civil litigants. The Guidelines also do not and probably will never provide broad and predictable protection to the researcher. They generally rely on ad hoc balancing of interests by the prosecutor. Further, prosecutorial guidelines are not judicially enforceable, leaving much discretion in the hands of the chief prosecutor within a particular jurisdiction. Finally, prosecutorial guidelines would not provide a uniform standard of protection, as different law enforcement agencies serve each of the states and the federal jurisdiction.

THE POWER TO LEGISLATE

Introduction

Statutes to protect researchers from compelled disclosure of information could be legislated in two ways. First, each jurisdiction--federal and state--could formulate its own legislation applicable only within its jurisdictional boundaries. For example, a New York statute would apply only to grand jury and legislative investigations and judicial proceedings held under the authority of New York State. Similarly, a federal statute would apply only to investigations and adjudicative proceedings authorized by the federal government.

The second possibility is that the federal government could provide legislation that would pertain to state as well as federal investigative and adjudicative proceedings. Such a statute could preempt or displace any state statutes that purport to grant similar protection; or, the federal statute could apply in full force to the federal system, but merely provide a minimum privilege that the states would be free to expand but not contract.

State v. Federal

Separate and Federal Legislation

The states have been the traditional forum in which established testimonial privileges[101] applicable in state proceedings have been instituted, either through the common law or through specific statutes. No constitutional issue is, thus, raised by the states instituting further privileges; state courts and legislatures have plenary power over the procedures of state adjudicative and investigative proceedings. (And, as well, can confer to certain relationships a privileged status.)

Similarly, Congress has plenary jurisdiction over federal investigative and adjudicative procedures and has, in the past, established privileges, albeit extremely narrow ones.[102] As for broader privileges, analogous to the traditional state-enacted privileges,[103] in the absence of the passage of the Proposed Federal Rules of Evidence[104] the federal courts have generally relied on common law as interpreted by the federal judiciary.[105]

Need for Uniformity

Despite the traditional practice in which the federal and state jurisdictions separately determine whether a privilege exists, the nature of research demands a uniform national rule. Research takes place in a context that transcends state lines. The subject of a great deal of research involves problems of national magnitude, such as drug abuse, crime, poverty, and American foreign policy.

There is a national interest in the fruits of research and, thus, in allowing researchers to work with the least possible inhibitions. If researchers are not protected, the negative impact will fall upon the entire nation, rather than on the inhabitants of one particular jurisdiction.

Furthermore, researchers are not generally limited to a particular jurisdiction for sources of information. If one jurisdiction offers the researcher protection while another does not, the entire project may be jeopardized. An investigative or adjudicative body of the jurisdiction that provides for no privilege may subpoena information relating to the entire scope of the project. Without a uniform law, researchers could not be assured that they would escape compelled disclosure of information and would refrain from controversial, yet socially important, subjects of inquiry. Also, in our mobile society, information about researchers' subjects may be desired by investigative or adjudicative bodies of a jurisdiction other than that in which the research is taking place. In this situation, also, the lack of national protection might cause researchers to avoid controversial areas of inquiry. Finally, information gathered by a researcher may be subject to compelled disclosure to investigative and adjudicative bodies on both the federal and state level.[106] Researchers cannot pursue controversial areas of inquiry if they know that, while they are protected from compelled disclosure on the federal level, state agencies may be able to hold them in contempt for refusal to disclose, or vice versa.

Basis for Congressional Action

An issue that must be considered is whether Congress has the authority to enact a statute that would protect researchers from subpoenas or other compulsory legal process issued on the state as well as federal levels. Three constitutional sources of authority will be discussed here: the First Amendment; the Commerce Clause; and the Necessary and Proper Clause.

The First Ammendment

As was discussed earlier, researchers are normally not protected by the First Amendment.[107] Branzburg v. Hayes limited, though did not totally reject, the applicability of the First Amendment to the news gathering and thus the information gathering process.[108] The Court, for example, left room for Congress to find that the burden that compulsory process inflicts upon news and information gathering cannot be overridden or outweighed by "the public interest in law enforcement and in insuring grand jury proceedings."[109]

The authority for Congress to enact legislation that carries out policies embodied in the First Amendment stems from section 5 of the Fourteenth Amendment.[110] The U.S. Supreme Court in Katzenbach v. Morgan[111] stated that section 5 is a positive grant of legislative authority, allowing Congress to determine what legislation is necessary to carry out the substance of the Fourteenth Amendment.[112] This authority is broad[113] and includes the power to legislate for the states[114] as well as the federal government.

In Katzenbach the court held congressional legislation[115] valid as a proper exercise of section 5 of the Fourteenth Amendment because the statute implemented the Equal Protection Clause of the Fourteenth Amendment.[116] Similarly, Congress can, pursuant to section 5 of the Fourteenth Amendment, implement the Due Process Clause of the Fourteenth Amendment. The Due Process Clause has long been held to "incorporate" the freedoms embodied in the First Amendment.[117] Congress, therefore, presumably has the power to fashion legislation such as a testimonial researcher's privilege to ensure that the First Amendment rights of researchers are not infringed. Such legislation would apply both on the federal and state levels.[118]

The Commerce Clause

The Commerce Clause[119] has been interpreted to grant Congress the broad power to regulate any activity that "affects commerce" among the several states.[120] Once federal power attaches under the Commerce Clause, it extends to all aspects of the activity, notwithstanding the degree of connection with interstate commerce or the fact that a connection with commerce had not actually been shown. Furthermore, legislation enacted pursuant to the Commerce Clause, applies equally to the federal and state jurisdictions. When interstate commerce is involved, the states cannot negate the supreme power of Congress.[121]

Enhanced by the Necessary and Proper Clause,[122] Congress has justified a wide variety of legislation with the Commerce Clause.[123] Of particular relevance is the fact that legislation regulating various locally based media, such as local radio and television[124] stations and local newspapers,[125] have been justified by the fact that these media are in commerce.

It is, thus, possible, pursuant to the Commerce and Necessary and Proper Clauses, for Congress to pass legislation to enhance the flow of information through media. The Commerce Clause could, therefore, justify a researcher's privilege if researchers distributed or intended to distribute (at even a remote time) their results via radio, television, newspapers, magazines, journals, and books. Researchers who merely disseminate information by face-to-face communication with their students, however, pose a problem under the commerce power rationale. Arguably, however, such individuals could be constitutionally covered by a federal researcher's privilege if Congress were to find that they are in or affect commerce in even some minute way.[127]

Necessary and Proper Clause: Federal Research

A third basis for the constitutional authority of Congress to legislate a statute to protect researchers against compulsory disclosure of information is the congressional power to pass laws that are "necessary and proper"[128] to carry out legitimate governmental functions.

If research is done under federal auspices and Congress finds that a researcher's privilege is needed to foster this activity, Congress may enact such legislation. Such a statute would protect researchers involved in "federal" research from compulsory legal process issued by both state and federal agencies.[129]

The term "federal" means some involvement of the national government through either the executive, legislative, or judicial branch. Two ways in which an individual or program can function as an instrumentality of the federal government can be identified. Programs and individuals that are supported in whole or in part by funds which emanate from the national government may be viewed as federal. Also, in the absence of federal funding, programs carrying out an enunciated policy of the national government may be federal. Funding by the national government will be considered first.

Clearly, research that is completely funded pursuant to a federal statute providing money for federal agencies is federal. The research activity of employees of a federal agency such as the Department of Health, Education, and Welfare is an obvious example. Also within the realm of federal activity is research undertaken by individuals, corporations, universities, and state and local governments pursuant to contracts and subcontracts with or grants from the U.S. Government.[130]

Research undertaken for a particular purpose, identified with a state, locality, private individual, or corporation supported in whole or in part, directly or indirectly, by funds of the federal government may be federal in some situations and may not be in others. No absolute rule has been set out by which to make this detemination. Three parameters, however, can be identified by which to consider whether the allocation of federal funds renders a particular research project "federal" and thereby subject to legislation passed pursuant to the Necessary and Proper Clause. One is the quantitative degree to which the federal funds support the activity;[131] the second is the degree of federal interest in the activity funded;[132] finally, the importance of the federal government's interest in regulating the particular activity funded can be considered.[133]

In considering a particular research activity, funded in some degree by the federal government in relation to these three factors, it is to be noted that each need not be present to a great degree. For example, if the quantity of federal funding is comparatively low, it can be counterbalanced by a strong federal interest in the type of activity funded.[134] In the context of deciding whether a particular research activity is federal for the purpose of granting the researcher protection against compulsory disclosure of information, the strong First Amendment interest inherent in the protection would probably offset minimal amounts of federal funding and somewhat insignificant federal interest in the subject matter of the research.

In sum, it is likely that a congressional statute that protects researchers from compulsory disclosure of information would apply to a large portion of research that is supported in some way by federal funds. Empirically, such a statute would protect a significant portion of the research activity pursued in the United States, for an increasingly large amount of research receives federal financing. For example, the federal government in 1968 spent $300,000,000 or 35 percent of the total $805,000,000 spent on social science research and development. This represented a sevenfold increase in federal expenditures on social research, up from $40,000,000 in 1958.[135]

The second means by which research activity can be considered "federal" is if, in the absence of any federal funding, the research significantly carries out a specific policy enunciated by a branch of the national government.[136] The Comprehensive Drug Abuse Prevention and Control Act of 1970 is directly relevant. It grants the Secretary of Health, Education, and Welfare[137] and the U.S. Attorney General[138] the power to authorize individuals engaged in research on the use and effect of drugs a privilege against compelled testimony. The legislative history of these sections makes it clear that "this [authority of the Secretary of Health, Education, and Welfare and the U.S. Attorney General] is not limited to research conducted and supported by the Federal government." This is because any such research accords with the national policy enunciated in the 1970 Drug Abuse Act.[139]

Preemption or Minimum Federal Standard

Assuming that a federal statute protecting researchers in state and federal proceedings can be enacted on the basis of the First Amendment, Commerce Clause, or Necessary and Proper Clause, should the statute provide a minimum degree of protection which the states can increase but not decrease,[140] or should it preempt all state legislation in the field?[141]

A federal statute that offers broad protection to a wide class of researchers should preempt the states from legislating in the area. Such a statute would negate the need for increased protection by the states. It would also ensure uniformity throughout the nation, necessary because research activity progresses in a national context. Researchers would be able to readily predict the degree of protection that the statute assures them in any jurisdiction. The interest in uniformity and ability of researchers to know exactly how the statute will protect them throughout the nation could generally outweigh the individual states' ability to further protect researchers where narrow exceptions are made in the federal statute.

On the other hand, if the federally enacted statute covers a limited class of researchers and provides for broad and, perhaps, ambiguous exceptions, the states should be allowed to enact their own statutes to grant researchers increased protection. The federal statute would merely serve as the minimum. The interest in granting researchers wider and more effective protection from compelled disclosure of information would outweigh the interest in national uniformity.

COVERAGE: PEOPLE

Introduction

Perhaps the most difficult task in drafting a statute to protect researchers from compelled disclosure of information is the formulation of a definition of the term "researcher."[142] In drafting a definition of a "researcher," the author must reconcile competing considerations. On the one hand, the definition must be sufficiently broad to include all individuals who legitimately are involved in the research process. On the other, the definition must not be so broad as to immunize society at large from its obligation to supply information in adjudicative and investigative proceedings,[143] subjecting the statute to constant abuse.

Furthermore, the definition must be carefully and unambiguously worded to permit those interpreting the statute and those seeking its protection to decide without undue difficulty if an individual is protected. Finally, as noted in the preceding section, if the statute is to be enacted by the federal government to apply both on federal and state levels, it must be possible for either the Commerce Clause, the First Amendment, or both to serve as the authority for the legislation.

Types of Definitions

At least four approaches to defining the researcher are possible.[144] They are listed in a continuum, ranging from a single word without definition and qualification to a functional approach.

1. The individuals covered by the statute could be defined by using a noun without further explanation of the term. This approach has often been used in statutes protecting "reporters" or professional journalists without any definition or enumerated criteria.[145] Unfortunately, this simple mode of specifying the individuals protected by the statute is seriously ambiguous.

2. Certain types of information collected in the course of a specific type of research might elevate coverage of the statute. One statute, for example, makes inadmissible under certain circumstances "records of the identity, diagnosis, prognosis or treatment" of patients that are maintained in the course of drug research.[146] This type of coverage, while perhaps the least ambiguous of all, has the vice of being extremely narrow. In the first place, it specifically immunizes researchers from producing certain types of records but does not explicitly cover the situation in which they are compelled to give oral testimony. While such wording would probably protect an individual from oral testimony on the contents of the specified records, protection would not extend beyond this limited protection, for example, to cover personal observations. This approach is more appropriate for statutes designed to protect a narrow category of researchers rather than researchers in general.

3. The definition could specify some type of relationship between the person protected and a specific type of research activity. An example would be extending protection to "persons engaged in research in the use and effect of drugs."[147] This approach has the advantage of probably extending coverage

to all individuals who have access to the data gathered in the research process; "engaged in" encompasses a wider range of individuals than the term "researcher" alone.[148] It, however, is most applicable to statutes that, rather than attempting to cover a broad spectrum of types of research, are limited to one particular category of research.[149]

4. The definition of individuals covered by the statute could focus on the way in which researchers function in relation to their work and society. No existing statute specifically granting a privilege to researchers has yet adopted this functional approach.[150] A number of existing state and proposed federal shield laws for journalists, however, employ this method.[151] In many instances these statutes extend coverage to a wide class of persons, including individuals traditionally viewed to be researchers rather than journalists.[152] For example, one statute--primarily intended to cover journalists--protects individuals who handle information for the purpose of "transmission, dissemination, or publication to the public."[153]

The functional approach is advocated here and is incorporated in the definitional scheme of the proposed Statute.[154] The functional approach is desirable because it allows protection to be conferred on all individuals who perform in a specified way and serve a particular role. It obviates many problems of ambiguity caused by granting protection to "researchers" or "scholars." It permits broad coverage, allowing individuals involved in all fields of inquiry, ranging, for example, from biological and medical sciences to behavioral sciences, to be covered by the Statute if their activities come within the specified pattern of behavior.[155] Finally, the functional approach allows protection to extend to all individuals who are involved in the research process, rather than only to the research team or to the person who actually gathers the information.

Who is a Researcher?

In fields such as law, medicine, or psychology in which privileges have been established, it is a relatively easy task to extend coverage to all members of the profession while not immunizing society at large.[156] These professions have strict licensing requirements.

But for researchers, as for journalists, there are no licensing requirements. In fact, serious First Amendment infringements would result if only those who acquired a state license could function as journalists or researchers.[157] A statute designed to protect researchers must, therefore, contain additional criteria that extend coverage only to bona fide researchers. It would be convenient if researchers could be defined in terms of a single element, such a membership in a professional organization or affiliation with a university as faculty member or research assistant.[158] Such an approach would exclude from coverage individuals who are actually engaged in important and, perhaps, controversial research but who are not affiliated with the research establishment.[159] These individuals may, in fact, need extra protection, for they often will not have the reputation and institutional backing that may be instrumental in fighting a subpoena.

Employing Standards Accepted in the Field of Inquiry

The proposed Statute sacrifices some degree of specificity and preciseness to accommodate all those who have a bona fide involvement with research activity. It extends coverage to individuals who in some way deal with information "obtained employing principles recognized or standards accepted in the field of inquiry." This requirement does not necessarily mean that an individual must employ the rigorous academic standards that may be prescribed by organizations established in a particular discipline. Nor does it mean that the individual must be engaged in research relating to established fields of academia. These factors may, however, be relevant in establishing a bona fide involvement in research. The Statute does, however, require that, at a minimum, the information that is sought by the subpoena or other legal process be obtained with a bona fide interest in its utilization in some type of rigorous investigation.

Within the environment of a specific research endeavor, the Statute attempts to extend protection to all people who ordinarily have access to information obtained in the course of the investigation, whether they gather, compile, store, analyze, review, edit, disseminate, or publish the material.[160] Research is often a group effort with all those involved working closely together and having access to the same information. It would be meaningless to allow the leader of the research team or the person who actually acquires the information to be granted immunity from compelled disclosure, while subjecting others who have access to the information to compulsory process.

The term "researcher" also applies to an individual who at the time of the contact with the information sought by subpoena or legal process qualified as a "researcher" but who no longer can be so described. If such coverage is not made explicit or implicit (as in the proposed Statute) in the privilege granting statute, an inequitable situation would result. Individuals handling research data would be subject to subpoena or other legal process once they terminated their roles as researchers.[161]

For Purposes of Public Benefit

Statutory protection is limited by the requirement that the research activity have purpose of benefit to the public.[162] This requirement is to be liberally construed. It is not necessary that the information sought have a specific public benefit of its own, nor is it required that the information ultimately be used to better society in some way. Before a socially useful breakthrough, a large amount of research must be done. Also, the phrase "public benefit" should not be subject to partisan interpretation, allowing protection only to researchers whose work appears to be furthering the goals of the political party presently in the majority or of the bureaucrats who presently control administrative agencies.

The information sought need only be obtained by a researcher for the purpose of serving the interests of society. This is in contrast to research done solely for the internal use of a profit-making entity. Socially beneficial research is often pursued by individuals and business entities intent upon making private financial profits. This is especially true of drug research and economic analysis. To exclude from coverage all research that is done in the course of profit-making endeavors would inhibit an important source of socially beneficial information. If the research pursued in the course of making profit is made available to the public,[163] it may be protected by the proposed Statute. If, on the other hand, the research is done solely for internal use and is not generally available,[164] it is not protected.

The public benefit requirement is necessary to square the Statute with the First Amendment. As was discussed earlier, the First Amendment is an important source of constitutional power for Congress to enact a privilege that would apply equally on national and state levels. The First Amendment is available as a source of congressional power only to the extent to which there is a probability or potentiality that the information will be communicated to the public. The public benefit requirement attempts to draft into the Statute this theoretical limit on the extent of the First Amendment without restricting coverage to research data disseminated in a particular manner.

Furthermore, there is a limit to the First Amendment's protection of "commercial speech." The U.S. Supreme Court has made it clear in a series of decisions[165] that speech that does nothing more than propose a commercial transaction is not protected by the First Amendment. Constitutional protection, therefore, would not seemingly extend to research data compiled by a commercial institution only for its internal use.

As a practical matter, the public benefit requirement will not sacrifice to a significant degree the protection granted by the Statute. While predictability of coverage may be decreased, it will be minimal. Most individuals will be able to determine whether the research in which they are involved will in some significant way benefit society or whether it is purely being done for the internal use of private profit-making concerns. Only in a small number of cases will the researcher have to rely on the courts for a final determination of this issue. Also, the interests served in making this requirement outweigh the de minimus loss of predictability.[166] For example, there is interest that the government should not make laws that benefit the private interests of a small class of individuals. This is especially true in granting a testimonial privilege. A statutory testimonial privilege for a particular group deprives other individuals of the important right to muster evidence in their favor in the contexts of civil or criminal investigative or adjudicative proceedings. Therefore, the legislature must counterbalance the limited deprivation of evidence with an important interest of the society at large.

In connection with the public benefit requirement, it should be noted that the protection of the proposed researcher privilege Statute, unlike many statutes for journalists,[167] is not limited to persons associated with specifically enumerated media, such as newspapers, magazines, radio, television, cable television, etc. It thus is not subject to the narrow interpretation that courts have applied in denying protection to an individual not affiliated with the statutory list of protected media but affiliated with a similar form of media.[168] Rather, the Statute merely requires that a significant purpose of the researcher's work be that it is pursued for public benefit. Communication to the public in any particular way is not required.

The proposed Statute, however, does employ the term "media" in its definition of a researcher.[169] The term "researcher" includes any individual who is involved in disseminating research data through any media. "Media" is broadly defined in the Statute to include any published or unpublished means by which research is reported.[170]

MATERIAL COVERED

A second issue that must be addressed by a statute to protect researchers from compelled disclosure of information is what types of information should be protected. This discussion, along with the related sections of the proposed Statute, applies equally to a statute designed to protect researchers in general and to one that is more limited, e.g., covering only federal evaluation research.

"In the Course of Research" Requirement

As has been emphasized, the proposed Statute is designed to foster social interests and constitutional mandates that relate to research activity in American society. The Statute aims at shielding individuals who qualify as "researchers" from their obligation as citizens to provide evidence in criminal and civil proceedings <u>only</u> when the information sought was obtained as part of a research activity. All researcher[171] and journalist[172] privilege statutes incorporate some type of requirement that the researcher or journalist be protected only within the course of gathering news or research data. The proposed Statute includes language restricting coverage to information handled "in the course of"[173] research activity.

The "in the course of" requirement, therefore, excludes from protection individuals otherwise qualifying as "researchers," but who--while off the job--at home or on vacation observe criminal activity, accidents, or other occurrences that may be relevant to investigative or adjudicative proceedings. In this way researchers are distinguished from other citizens only when they are performing a function that has a significant social benefit. It should be noted that the "in the course of" requirement must be distinguished from a requirement that one be presently engaged as a researcher at the time the privilege is asserted. The latter type of requirement is specifically rejected by the proposed Statute.[174]

Requirement of Confidentiality

A major step in the process of behavioral research is the gathering of various types of information from and about people. The subjects of a research endeavor are those "individuals whose actions or responses are being studied."[175]

The proposed Statute extends protection from compelled disclosure to all information received and observed in the course of studying the actions or responses of human beings, whether or not an explicit or implicit promise of confidentiality has been made by the researcher to the subject.[176] The absence of a requirement of a promise of confidentiality in order to evoke the privilege serves all parties who have an interest in a research privilege statute.

First of all, the subjects' interests in keeping the invasion of their privacy to a minimum and in making sure that the information they supply will not be the basis for prosecution or reprisal can only be adequately fostered if the statute's protection is not conditioned on a promise of confidentiality. This can be illustrated by examining the nature of the researcher-subject relationship as well as the various methodologies employed in the course of behavioral research.

Unlike the news informant[177] who often comes forward with information to the reporter upon the condition that her or his identity or certain facts remain confidential, the research subject is generally sought after by the researcher. The subject rarely volunteers information, conditioning it on a promise of confidentiality. Also, the anonymous citizens, likely subjects of many research projects, often lack the experience of public figures in dealing with demands for information made by researchers. Their understanding of the concept of consent is not sophisticated and they may often presume that the information they supply will not be turned over to the "authorities"[178] and, thus, be confidential.[179] Notwithstanding serious ethical problems of consent and confidentiality in research,[180] the protection of the subject should thus not be conditioned upon the fortuitous circumstance of whether or not the researcher specifically promises that the information will be confidential. The <u>expectation of confidentiality</u> on the part of subjects should dictate that the statute be operative whether or not an explicit or implicit promise of confidentiality has been made.

At least three traditional methodologies of behavioral research[181] often preclude explicit or even implicit promises of confidentiality.

1. <u>Self-description by the subject elicited through interviews, personality tests, and questionnaires.</u> It is possible that even the best intentioned researcher may not provide a promise of confidentiality. Also, questionnaires and personality tests may be so constructed as to elicit information that subjects ordinarily would not divulge. Such information should not be subject to compelled testimony, whether or not assurances of confidentiality are made.

2. <u>Direct observation and recording of individual behavior.</u> Research designs that involve observation of individuals through one-way mirrors, participation in a group, and observation of the specific behavior of individuals in public places provide little or no opportunity for the researcher to make any assurance of confidentiality or for the subject to demand such an assurance. Often, the mere revelation that the subjects are being observed, such as in studies of homosexual behavior in public places, may frustrate the entire research project. The ethical transgressions that may be involved in pursuing observational research without the consent of the subjects are greatly compounded if a researcher is compelled to disclose information obtained in the course of research because no promise of confidentiality was made. The subject's privacy interest would be assaulted on two levels: being observed for research purposes without consent and the possible reporting of these observations in investigative and adjudicative proceedings.

3. <u>Descriptions of one person by another serving as an informant and the use of secondary data such as health, education, welfare, or court records.</u> Third-party descriptions of an individual can severely infringe upon the privacy rights of the person described. To subject this information to compelled disclosure only because no promise of confidentiality was made would compound the infringement on the privacy interests of both the informant and the subject. The use of records maintained by hospitals, schools, social welfare agencies,

or courts for independent research purposes is an assault on the subject's privacy. It is compounded by subjecting records to compelled disclosure if the researcher did not receive them under a promise of confidentiality. Furthermore, the individual described by the informant or record rarely is in a position to demand a promise of confidentiality as a condition for the researcher receiving the information. A promise of protection will, thus, generally depend upon the informant or person who controls the records asking for assurance of confidentiality or the researcher volunteering such a promise. The person jeopardizing the subject's privacy is not within the subject's control.

The interests of the parties who have a stake in the quality of research are, also, fostered by the absence of a requirement of confidentiality. As was discussed, methodologies employed by behavioral researchers often make it difficult to provide for an opportunity to extend an explicit or even implicit promise of confidentiality to the subject. The quality of research, however, is both dependent on the availability of these methodologies as research tools and on protection from compelled disclosure of information.[182] Maximum protection from investigative and adjudicative subpoenas and other legal process can, thus, only be provided if a promise of confidentiality is not a condition precedent for statutory protection.

Finally, the interest in providing a statute that can be administered without undue litigation is served by not requiring that a promise of confidentiality be made in order for the researcher to be protected from compulsory disclosure.[183] The factual issue of whether a promise of confidentiality was, in fact, made or even implied presents difficult problems of proof. The difficulty is most severe in situations where the researcher does not want to reveal the identity of the subject. To make the subject testify as to whether an express or implied promise of confidentiality was made would be to severely risk revealing the subject's identity. This is notwithstanding procedural precautions, such as closed hearings. On the other hand, if the researcher's testimony, alone, is sufficient to establish the existence of a promise of confidentiality, the requirement is self-serving and meaningless. In cases where the content of the information and not the identity of the source is to be confidential, it is likely that both the researcher and the subject will desire statutory protection from compelled disclosure. The testimony of both these individuals may, thus, be self-serving. Apart from research designs that provide for written assurances of confidentiality, or obvious indicia that confidentiality is implied, the difficulty in proving the existence of such an assurance can lead to unwarranted prolonged litigation. This litigation may not in many cases result in a reliable determination of the issue.[184]

Identity of the Subject

The identity of the source of information and the contents of any information that could reasonably reveal the source's identity is the most common type of information protected by statutes granting privileges to researchers[185] and journalists.[186] The proposed Statute similarly protects this information from compelled disclosure.

Concealing the identity of subjects is a concern of virtually all researchers who deal with human subjects. The problems and issues relating to protecting the identity of subjects from compelled disclosure differ, depending on the type of subjects involved. Research subjects range from public officials and informants on public events to individuals having no public notoriety.

Researchers, in the course of investigating sensitive public issues, depend on information from sources similar to those relied on by investigative reporters.[187] These researchers have been referred to as "public scholars" and have been identified as serving a vital function in society.[188] Because of their similarity to reporters, the necessity to protect the identity of their sources parallels the reporters' need. When the subject's identity is vulnerable to compulsory process, first-hand informants dry up. Also, the quality of the relationship between the researcher and the subject in terms of the subject's candor and spontaneity is likely to decrease.[189] Richard Barnet, author and political scientist, testified to the need for statutory protection against disclosure of the identity of subjects relied on by public scholars:

> No public official will risk giving information if he fears that the scholar will be compelled to expose him before a grand jury or in court. Unless first amendment privileges apply as well to the public, he will be effectively precluded from studying the very sensitive areas of public policy which the public most crucially needs to be informed.[190]

Unlike journalists, many researchers rely heavily on observing human behavior and eliciting responses about personal matters from individuals in all walks of life; researchers are often interested in investigating matters that relate to the day-to-day life and opinions of society at large or of segments of society. The data gathered through this type of research are generally used to provide a collective statistical picture of such matters as the occurrence of particular practices in society, the causes for such practices, the effect of certain governmental and private inputs on society, and the opinion of society on specific issues that are often controversial.[191] The reporting of this information generally does not reflect the identity of the subjects. The researcher, however, often has access to the identity of the subjects. The linking of the identity of a particular subject and his or her personal responses or actions can be useful in the course of investigative and adjudicative proceedings, having purposes different from that of the research.[192]

Researchers have recognized that if the identity of the non-public figures or officials to whom they have turned for information is subject to compelled disclosure, their research would be severely jeopardized. Subjects would be far less willing to provide candid responses to personal and controversial questions, often necessary in the course of research. Furthermore, researchers themselves would be reluctant on ethical grounds to conduct studies requiring personal responses or the observation of human behavior,[193] for an unjustifiable burden on the privacy of the subject[194] would result. Important research on our society's collective behavior and views would be stifled.

A number of designs have been developed by researchers in response to the need to ensure that the identity of subjects remain confidential.[195] These, however, are not adequate in all cases to insulate the identity of subjects from the power of investigative and adjudicative bodies to compel testimony.[196] The only sure protection from compelled disclosure of the identity of research subjects in the context of the type of research under discussion is a statutory provision specifically immunizing this information.

Contents of Communications with a Subject

The contents of information received from a subject can theoretically be distinguished from the subject's identity. In practice, however, this is difficult, as the two are often closely related. For example, the substance of the information compiled by a public scholar may, by its nature, point directly to a single subject or a small number of possible subjects; these may be the only individuals who could possibly have had access to the information at hand. Only some of the existing research privilege statutes[197] and existing and proposed privilege statutes[198] for journalists protect the contents of information supplied by the informant. In contrast, virtually all such statutes protect the identity of the source.

The proposed Statute opts in favor of protecting the contents of information received from a source. One reason for granting this protection is the practical difficulty in distinguishing between the information per se and information that would reasonably reveal the identity of the source. Because there is a substantial risk that upon compelled disclosure of the contents of the communication the identity of the subject will be revealed, it is desirable to broadly protect this information. Furthermore, those individuals who are familiar with the subject or who have access to further information about the subject are likely to be able to connect information supplied by the subject with the subject's identity. It is these individuals who are generally in a position to take recourse against the subject on learning that information was revealed.

Another reason for protecting information revealed by the subject is to allow researchers the discretion to disclose information at a time when they believe it will not be used detrimentally against those who supplied it. The contents of the communication may reveal sensitive material on a segment of the population. For example, the information may identify a particular group as being involved in criminal activity. If this is subject to compelled disclosure, the researcher's ability to find willing subjects within the community would greatly decrease despite the fact that the source's identity is protected.

Direct Observations of Subjects

Much research involving human subjects is accomplished by observing behavior and activities, as noted in the earlier discussion on confidentiality. Absent explicit coverage of researchers' personal observations of their subjects, a court may, as in the news area, narrowly construe the statute to exclude from protection this type of information. For example, in the Branzburg[199] litigation, Paul Branzburg, a reporter, was subpoenaed to reveal to a grand jury the identity of persons observed by him converting marijuana into hashish. These observations formed the basis of his article. The court, despite the fact that Branzburg had promised to maintain a confidential relationship with those involved, ruled that the applicable Kentucky statute,[200] protecting a reporter's "source of information," did not extend protection to activities that the reporter personally observed. In the context of direct observations, the reporter, not any individual participant, was viewed as the source of information. Branzburg was thus compelled to reveal the identity of those involved.[201] The proposed Statute, therefore, specifically protects information "observed" by the researcher.[202]

It is important that the observations of the researcher be protected. It is possible that the researcher will gain access to the observation of certain activities based on the subject's permission to do so. Without the subject, the researcher would not have known or have been permitted to observe the relevant information. To allow this information to be amenable to compelled disclosure may have a damaging effect on the researcher's ability to maintain working relationships with valuable subjects. Also, whether or not a particular subject directed the researcher to observe specific behavior or activity, to subject this information to compelled disclosure would be to potentially chill the researcher's desire to employ the observational technique in studying controversial modes of behavior. Society's ability to learn about itself would subsequently be inhibited. Finally, compelling disclosure of the researcher's observations may be a logical first step in the subpoenaing agency's quest to learn the identity of subjects who are engaged in illegal activity.

Work Product

The research process often extends over a long period of time. During the course of their work, researchers are likely to compile voluminous notes, memoranda, and preliminary drafts, which--absent a privilege--may be subject to compelled disclosure. This material is analogous to the work product of the attorney in preparing a client's case, described by the Supreme Court in the leading case, Hickman v. Taylor,[203] as including "interviews, statements, memoranda, correspondence, briefs, mental impressions, personal beliefs and countless other tangible and intangible ways.[204] The attorney-client privilege protects from compulsory process both the attorney's communications with the client and the attorney's work product.

While no researcher privilege statute explicitly extends protection to work product, a few existing state[205] and proposed federal privilege statutes for journalists[206] do. The proposed Statute seeks to protect the researcher's work product from compelled disclosure.[207]

The need to protect the work product is threefold. In the first place, if the work product were not protected, the anonymity of the subject, contents of communications with the subject, and observations of the researcher would be jeopardized. Investigative and adjudicative agencies could compel disclosure of the researcher's work product, which would probably reveal these other types of information. Secondly, researchers should be encouraged rather than discouraged to record in writing or on tape, film, or other information storing device, their preliminary findings, ideas, and tentative conclusions. This will help add to the efficiency and enhance the quality of their work, ultimately benefiting the public. In this sense, the research process itself depends on statutory protection. Finally, like the protection granted to an attorney's work product by the Federal Rules of Criminal Procedure[208] and the Federal Rules of Civil Procedure,[209] the researcher's work product should not be available to law enforcement agencies or parties in litigation to obviate their need to do their own investigation. Researchers may be reluctant to pursue controversial areas if they know that their work will be used for unintended purposes. Justice Powell, concurring in Branzburg, in fact recognized that news media (ergo, researchers) should not serve law enforcement agencies:

> Certainly we do not hold . . . that state and federal authorities are free to "annex" the news media as an investigative arm of the government.[210]

The proposed Statute attempts to extend coverage to all forms in which researchers maintain their work product by protecting any information storing device, object, or thing.[211] If the Statute were silent as to information storage, a court may narrowly construe the Statute to protect only information stored in particular forms. For example, it may limit coverage to written material only or may exclude from protection unprocessed information, such as undeveloped film. Existing broad research[212] and journalist[213] statutes generally do not specify the forms of information that are protected.

The proposed Statute, on the other hand, broadly and explicitly defines the term "information storing device."[214] It is intended to include all methods of recording or storing processed or unprocessed information. The researcher is immunized from being compelled to give testimony (subpoena ad testifacdum) or to produce any information storing device, object, or thing (subpoena duces tecum).

This extension of protection to all means by which researchers retain the information they have gathered allows researchers to be free to pursue all types of research designs and methodologies. They are not forced to defensively store their information in a limited number of forms enumerated by a narrow statute. Nor must they have to worry that an ambiguous statute will be interpreted so as not to grant protection.

SCOPE OF PROTECTION: POSSIBLE LIMITATIONS

Introduction

The proposed Statute as drafted provides for an "absolute"[215] privilege with a narrow exception for waiver. The following text discusses limitations that have been traditionally associated with privilege conferring statutes. Narrowly drawn exceptions are included for the situations when researchers are subpoenaed by criminal defendants and by parties involved in civil litigation.

Absolute or Qualified

The scope of protection granted by common law or statutory privileges has often been described as either absolute or qualified. An absolute privilege theoretically protects the beneficiaries of the privilege from compelled disclosure of specific types of information under all circumstances; a qualified privilege specifies circumstances under which the beneficiaries are not protected.

The absolute-qualified dichotomy is too rigid a conceptual framework from which to consider the scope of a privilege against compelled disclosure of information. In the first place, whether a privilege is qualified or absolute is often a question of degree, not kind. For example, a qualified privilege can protect 99 percent of all cases protected by an absolute privilege. On the other hand, it could deny protection to 99 percent of all cases. Secondly, it is difficult to imagine a privilege that is totally absolute. While the attorney-client privilege is generally viewed as providing absolute protection, for example, the presence of a third party or counselling on future crimes has traditionally rendered the privilege inoperative.[216] Also, all privileges are generally subject to waiver of some type. Furthermore, despite statutory language conferring an absolute privilege, courts may interpret the privilege so as to make it inoperative under certain circumstances. The court in In re WBAI-FM,[217] for example, decided that despite the absolute language of the New York privilege statute for journalists,[218] the protection granted to the press must yield to the overriding public policy of investigating crime, at least in cases where the information is passively received by the news media. Ironically, an absolute privilege may provide a court with a greater opportunity to carve out exceptions at its own discretion than a qualified privilege containing carefully limited exceptions.

In the interest of providing maximum protection for the researcher, the advocacy of an absolute privilege or no privilege at all is rejected. In order to provide the most effective privilege for researchers, two points should be considered: first, the statutory language should allow for maximum protection; second, the statute should make it clear to the researcher under what circumstances, if any, the privilege would be divested. A broad statute that is neither carefully drafted nor explained may not allow the researcher to predict with accuracy whether the courts will carve out qualifications to the privilege. On the other hand, a statute explicitly providing for broad ambiguous exceptions, such as where national security is involved, would not serve the goal of predictability nor would it provide on its face adequate protection for the researcher.

Ideally, a statute should be drafted with explicit language as well as commentary excluding all exceptions except waiver. Such a statute would serve both the interests of maximum protection and predictability.

As a second choice, a statute could be drafted with narrowly drawn exceptions, reflecting important countervailing interests. The researcher would have notice of the types of situations in which the privilege divested. Researchers could then, with some degree of accuracy, assess whether their work would be confronted with such a situation. If researchers believed that there was a high probability that an exception to the privilege would be operative in their case, they would attempt to devise defensive research methods at the onset to preclude disclosure of incriminating information about the subjects. If, however, this was impossible, the researchers would have to consider the ethical ramifications of going forward and might decide against pursuing the research. Furthermore, if the researcher were in a position to be compelled to disclose information, supplying the information would serve an important countervailing social interest. Such a statute with narrowly drawn exceptions reflecting important societal interests would be preferable to complete reliance on the First Amendment, which, in the face of Branzburg v. Hayes, is not much protection at all.

Judicial Balancing of Interests

One approach to qualifying a researcher's privilege is to allow a court to weigh various considerations in order to compare the impact of non-disclosure upon the party desiring the information with the effect of disclosure upon the research process. Such an approach is taken by the confidentiality provisions of the Drug Abuse, Office, and Treatment Act of 1972,[219] authorizing disclosure of records of the identity, diagnosis, prognosis, or treatment of patients engaged as subjects in drug research upon authorization by an

> . . . appropriate order of a court of competent jurisdiction granted after application showing good cause thereof. In assessing good cause the court shall weigh the public interest and the need for disclosure against the injury to the patient [subject], to the physician [researcher] patient relationship, and to the treatment services.[220]

A similar balancing approach is incorporated in two state journalist statutes.[221]

Allowing the judiciary to employ an ad hoc balancing test would produce results similar to having no statutory privilege at all and the researcher relying totally on the First Amendment as interpreted in Branzburg.[222] It is, thus, probable that in a criminal case the researcher's privilege would yield to both the prosecutorial interest in law enforcement and the Sixth Amendment rights of defendants. Because the researcher engaged in the study of criminal activity or behavior is particularly vulnerable to the compulsory process of investigative and adjudicative agencies,[223] a statutory balancing approach probably would not protect the type of research that most needs protection. While there would be greater possibility of protection in the context of civil cases, researchers' ability to predict their chances of coverage before embarking upon a particular project would be low. This is compounded by the improbability that researchers would be able to foresee that civil litigation will be dependent on the fruits of their research.

Utilizing an ad hoc judicial balancing standard is, therefore, rejected in the proposed draft. If any qualifications must be made in a researcher's privilege statute, the balancing should be accomplished at the legislative, not judicial, level. This will make it easier for the researcher and sponsoring agencies to predict whether or not their work is covered. It will also provide for more uniform application of the statute regardless of the judge deciding the case or the jurisdiction or venue in which the litigation takes place.

Proceedings Covered

Compulsory process can be exercised in the course of a variety of proceedings, including those of grand juries,[224] legislative committees,[225] administrative agencies,[226] and criminal[227] and civil courts.[228] Researcher and journalist statutes generally confer protection in all these proceedings either by specifically enumerating the proceedings[229] or by not mentioning any specific proceedings.[230] The scope of protection conferred, furthermore, is the same no matter in which proceeding the privilege is invoked.

It has been advocated[231] that the scope of protection should vary, depending on the context in which the privilege is invoked--either in investigative or adjudicative proceedings.[232] Investigative proceedings, exploratory in nature, rarely have a narrow focus; seldom does a single witness alter their outcome.[233] But investigative subpoenas are more damaging to journalists in causing sources to dry up than are adjudicative subpoenas. Sources resent a reporter's complicity with investigative proceedings that are perceived as partisan and vindictive. An absolute privilege to resist investigative subpoenas, therefore, would result in little evidentiary loss but would greatly foster the flow of information to the public.

It is advocated,[234] on the other hand, that adjudicative proceedings are generally apolitical and objective, deciding concrete disputes between identifiable persons. As such, they play a more important role in society than do investigative proceedings. They provoke less resentment among sources, making it less likely for sources to dry up.[235] Furthermore, the evidentiary loss by granting a single witness a privilege can have a significant effect on the outcome of the focused inquiry of a court adjudication. For adjudicative proceedings, an absolute privilege is advocated only for the identity of the source. As for the contents of the communication, a qualified privilege is recommended.[236]

The proposed Statute, drafted to provide maximum protection, confers the privilege in all proceedings that are empowered with compulsory process.[237] The privilege is of equal strength in all proceedings covered. The investigative-adjudicative distinction is of little relevance in the research context. Research subjects' perceptions of investigative proceedings as partisan and vindictive will generally have no bearing on their participation in a research project. Researchers, unlike journalists, often seek out their sources. Under certain circumstances, such as in evaluating federal welfare programs, subjects may feel obligated to respond to the researcher's questions for fear that the benefits will be terminated if they fail to respond. Also, researchers depend heavily on observational techniques in gathering information about their subjects. In this situation, subjects have little control over whether they are to be participants in the project.

Countervailing Interests

Law Enforcement Interests

Introduction. An exception carved out in a number of existing[238] and proposed privilege statutes for journalists[239] pertains to prosecutorial subpoenas. The journalist's privilege is divested if, for example, its operation results in a miscarriage of justice, the information relates to a threat to human life or national security, espionage, or to a probable violation of the law. The Supreme Court in Branzburg similarly recognized the law enforcement interest in requiring reporters to testify before grand juries and criminal proceedings:

> Fair and effective law enforcement aimed at providing
> security for person and property of the individual is
> a fundamental function of government and the grand jury

> plays an important, constitutionally mandated role in the
> process. On the records now before us we perceive no basis
> for holding that the public interest in law enforcement
> and in ensuring effective grand jury proceedings is in-
> sufficient to override the consequential, but uncertain,
> burden on news gathering that is said to result from in-
> sisting that reporters, like other citizens, respond to
> relevant questions put to them in the course of a valid
> grand jury investigation or criminal trial.[240]

Individuals directly involved in law enforcement activities have obviously recognized the interest that law enforcement agencies have in compelling reporters on at least some occasions to reveal information about criminal behavior within their possession. Robert G. Dixon, Jr., Assistant Attorney General, testified before the Subcommittee on Constitutional Rights of the U.S. Senate:

> The label of "newsman" should not serve as a shibboleth
> allowing the reporter who witnesses a bank robbery or
> receives notice of an alibi to conceal vital informa-
> tion relevant to the commission of a crime.[241]

The proposed Statute, however, rejects any exception designed to foster law enforcement interests.[242] As is pointed out by the reported incidents involving the subpoenaing of researchers,[243] the major reason that researchers are compelled to reveal information is in the furtherance of some law enforcement interest. Thus, to divest the privilege upon the requesting party's showing that a law enforcement interest is served would be to negate the effectiveness of the privilege. Furthermore, it is the intent of the proposed Statute to assure that researchers do not become investigative arms of prosecutors. Researchers generally pursue their work for purposes other than law enforcement. They are adverse to the use of their work for unintended purposes. Research that may lead to bettering our society through understanding and controlling criminal activity would, therefore, be inhibited by an exception to the privilege for law enforcement interests. Also, the vast investigative resources of law enforcement agencies as opposed to the comparatively meager investigative potential of most criminal defendants militates against the researcher becoming an investigative arm for law enforcement agencies.

National Security. A number of proposed statutes for journalists[244] and one researcher statute[245] specifically provide that the privilege be divested upon a showing that national security is involved. It is obvious that a nation has an interest in maintaining national security. This interest, in fact, can under certain circumstances override basic freedoms of the individual and can even justify discriminations based on race.[246] The interest of the nation in national security can, at times, similarly outweigh a researcher's statutory privilege based on the preservation of First Amendment interests.

The proposed Statute does not provide for an exception to the privilege for national security interests. National security is an ambiguous concept that could be abused by governmental agencies and prosecutors desiring information from researchers. The potential threat to any type of controversial research if a national security exception is provided is pointed out only too well by the activities in the Watergate incident, which were justified by participants as being in the interest of a distorted view of the national security. Activities as diverse as subverting the presidential campaign of George McGovern to the breaking in to the office of Daniel Ellsberg's psychiatrist were so justified. More analogous to the researcher situation is a case in which the national security exception to the confidentiality provisions of the Social Security Act was stated to justify revealing Social Security data to help track down draft evaders.[247] It is our belief that, absent a national security exception, if a situation arises when it is truly necessary to the very security of our nation that a researcher be compelled to testify, a court will override a privilege statute.

   <u>Prior Crimes</u>. The proposed researcher privilege Statute rejects as an exception information relating to crimes already committed. As in the news area,[248] it is unlikely that a researcher will possess information about crimes that law enforcement agencies view as most important to control, such as those offenses comprising the FBI's list of "index crimes": murder, rape, robbery, burglary, grand larceny, assault, and motor vehicle theft. Law enforcement agencies would, therefore, not generally obtain high priority information by compelling researchers to testify or produce information storing devices. Research investigations dealing with criminal behavior, in fact, often involve two types of activities, "victimless crimes"[249] or political corruption.[250]

   Society is better served if the researcher is allowed to freely study victimless crimes and political corruption and to provide information about their causes, their effects upon the individuals involved and upon society, as well as the incidence of this behavior and possible remedies. Absent some type of assurance that this information will be kept confidential, researchers will be loath to pursue these types of studies. Subjects, if fairly informed of the risks, will be reluctant to provide candid and frank responses. Some prosecutors, in fact, believe that society is better served if researchers are encouraged to freely study various types of criminal behavior rather than inhibiting research in order to obtain a single conviction here and there. George Van Hoomissen, the first Dean of the National Academy of District Attorneys, expressed such a view:

> While serving as District Attorney for Multnomah County, Oregon, 1962-1970, I had occasion from time to time to enter into rather informal agreements with individuals doing research primarily in the marijuana, dangerous drug and hard narcotics area. The researchers were naturally concerned that police or prosecution might seize or subpoena their records and thereby expose their informants to investigation and possible prosecution. Frankly, I was more concerned with the results of the research than with any possibility of prosecution.[251]

The question of whether to provide for the divestment of the privilege only when serious crimes are involved, such as those in the FBI index, necessarily arises. This has been advocated in the news area.[252] The proposed Statute, however, does not provide for this type of qualification.

   There are three basic ways in which researchers can compile information about serious crimes. Most commonly they acquire this information from subjects responding to interviews and questionnaires. Subjects are generally assured that they will remain anonymous. If no such assurance is made, subjects are likely to assume that anonymity will be maintained. People would not ordinarily incriminate themselves or implicate others in criminal behavior if they believe the information would be available for law enforcement purposes. An ethical researcher[253] similarly would not elicit this information unless assured of some safeguard of confidentiality.

A second method by which a researcher may be exposed to serious criminal behavior is through direct observation. It is unlikely that the researcher will be in a position to actually observe the serious criminal acts. If, however, researchers observe serious criminal activity during the course of their work, the Statute should help to resolve researchers' moral dilemma between their obligation to maintain their subjects' privacy and their obligation as citizens to report crime. Only if the dilemma is resolved in favor of protecting subjects' privacy can society hope to learn about crime from a behavioral science point of view, rather than from a law enforcement perspective. In the long run, society at large will benefit from offering the researcher such protection.

Finally, a researcher can inadvertently become a party to information relating to the identity of a suspect involved in a serious crime. Such a situation arose in People v. Newman.[254] A witness to a murder recognized the killer as a patient in a New York City methadone clinic. Pictures of the patients at the clinic, a drug research facility, were subpoenaed by the district attorney so that the criminal could be identified. Asserting a privilege under the confidentiality provisions of the Comprehensive Drug Abuse Prevention and Control Act,[255] the director of the methadone clinic refused to reveal the photographs. The New York Court of Appeals upheld the director's statutory researcher's privilege, reversing a lower court's contempt citation. When researcher's records containing identifying and personal information about individuals are kept for a purpose other than studying crimes or aiding law enforcement agencies, the researchers' primary obligation to the subjects is to make sure that the records are used only for their designated purpose. This is notwithstanding the need for such records in investigating serious crimes. A researcher privilege statute should assure researchers that they will be able to fulfill this obligation to their subjects. A qualification to the privilege for investigating serious criminal activity would undermine this important aspect of the statute's protection.

Future Crimes. No journalist or researcher statutes specifically exempt from protection information relating to crimes to be committed in the future. The proposed Statute, as well, makes no such qualification.

Concern for divesting the privilege in the context of information relating to future crimes stems from a traditional exception to the attorney-client privilege. It is settled law that the attorney-client privilege does not extend to communications between the attorney and the client that have as their purpose the furtherance of the client's future crimes.[256] An attorney advising a client as to future criminal activity would, in fact, be participating in a conspiracy rather than supplying legal advice. It would flaunt the purpose of the attorney-client privilege (the adequate provision of counsel) to allow this information privileged status.

In contrast to the attorney, the researcher does not gain knowledge of future crimes in the capacity of supplying advice to subjects. Hypothetically, a situation may arise in which the researcher studying the use and effect of drugs will become privy to information relating to a future drug-related crime, such as burglarizing a home to obtain money to purchase drugs. The researcher is a disinterested observer who has acquired the confidence of individuals involved in criminal activity; the researcher is not involved in preparing or planning for a crime, potentially resulting in conspiratorial liability. Knowledge of the future crime stems only from the subject's willingness to be candid in the researcher's presence. No perversion of justice would, therefore, result if a researcher were privileged to withhold information about future crimes.[257] On the other hand, the viability of the researcher-subject relationship, crucial to research about criminal behavior, will be fostered.[258] Subjects' interest in privacy and not incriminating themselves will be furthered as well as researchers' interest in avoiding the practical dilemma of whether to avoid a contempt citation and jail sentence by unethically foresaking their subjects' confidence.

Criminal Defendants: The Sixth Amendment Interest

No researcher and only a few journalist privilege statutes provide an exception to the protection in cases where a defendant subpoenas a researcher or reporter to testify on his or her behalf in a criminal trial.

A defendant's interest in compelling testimony in her or his favor is of the highest stature, for it is specifically protected in the Bill of Rights. The Sixth Amendment provides: "In all criminal prosecutions, the accused shall enjoy the right . . . to have compulsory process for obtaining witnesses in his favor."[259] The right has been described by the Supreme Court as follows:

> The right to offer testimony of witnesses and to compel their attendance if necessary, is in plain terms the right to present a defense . . . Just as the accused has a right to confront the prosecution's witnesses for the purpose of challenging their testimony, he has a right to present his own witnesses to establish a defense. This right is a fundamental element of due process.[260]

On a practical level, defendants' right to compel testimony in their favor helps to redress the imbalance in investigatory power they posses as compared to that of the prosecution. Indigents make up a large percentage of criminal defendants. They often lack the financial resources and the time to pursue an adequate investigation so as to prepare a competent defense in their favor.[261] The constitutional right to compel testimony, thus, is a most important element in the defendant's quest to adequately meet the prosecution's charges. The recent amendments to the Federal Rules of Criminal Procedure reflect the importance of the power of compulsory process to criminal defendants.[262]

In the context of defense subpoenas, therefore, a researcher's privilege statute is potentially in direct conflict with a constitutional right and an important investigatory device inherent to criminal defendants. Because the researcher's privilege statute has as its basis the First Amendment interest of providing the public with information,[263] the clash presented involves two constitutionally protected interests. The U.S. Supreme Court has not yet resolved this clash. However, lower federal and state courts have addressed the issue of the scope of the Sixth Amendment right to compel testimony and have resolved clashes between the defendant's Sixth Amendment right and opposing constitutional rights of the individuals subpoenaed. The Sixth Amendment right to subpoena witnesses has been described by the Wisconsin Supreme Court as "no more absolute than any of the other rights guaranteed by the constitution." It is thus not "unqualified."[264] In a clash between the two constitutional rights, the U.S. Ninth Circuit Court of Appeals held that the Fifth Amendment right against self incrimination of the defendant's accomplice outweighed the defendant's Sixth Amendment right to subpoena the accomplice.[265]

More in point, a federal district court in United States v. Liddy[266] decided in favor of a defendant's right to compel testimony in the context of a reporter's source. The court denied the Los Angeles Times' motion to quash trial subpoenas issued by a defendant in the Watergate criminal litigation, calling for tapes of interviews with the chief government witness. The newspaper asserted that the subpoenas should be quashed as infringements on the ability of journalists to gather information, protected by the First Amendment. The court emphasized the unique fact situation presented: the identity of the source was known; the information related to statements of a chief government witness; there was only a speculative infringement upon the news gathering activity; and the defendants had acted in good faith.[267] The court made it clear that "the decision will have little precedential value for defendants . . . who might wish to subject newspapers to an abusive 'flood of subpoenas.'"[268] The court, referring to the Branzburg denial of a reporter's privilege in favor of the public interest in law enforcement, reasoned that "while the public has a crucial interest in the investigation of criminal activity, it must have an even deeper interest in assuring that every defendant receive a fair trial."[269]

There is, thus, a possibility that a researcher's privilege statute, which in no way accommodates the defendant's Sixth Amendment interests, may, in fact, be held to violate the Constitution. The defendant's right to compulsory process may be held to override the First Amendment interest of the researcher in cases where the defendant acts in good faith in issuing the subpoena, the burden on the researcher's ability to gather is speculative, or the contents of the communication with subject or the observations of the subject rather than the subject's identity is demanded. In other situations, the non-absolute Sixth Amendment right to subpoena witnesses would probably be overridden by the researcher's First Amendment interests embodied in the proposed Statute.

The proposed Statute is designed specifically to protect those having an interest in the researcher's ability to resist subpoenas or other legal process. To this end, it is desirable that the privilege protect the researcher from defense subpoenas. An exception for defense subpoenas, no matter how narrowly drawn, would decrease researchers' ability to predict whether or not a situation will arise requiring them to reveal information. They may, therefore, decide against certain research projects. A draft of a narrow statutory exception for defense subpoenas, however, is provided because this may be constitutionally required. The exception is operative only if the defendant is acting in good faith in requesting the contents of communications or observations of the researcher. The identity of the researcher's subjects is not within the exception.

Defense Subpoena Exception

(a) A defendant in a criminal adjudicative proceeding may apply to the trial court for an order diverting the privilege conferred in section 2 of this Act provided that the application does not specify that the identity of a subject or information which would reasonably reveal the identity of a subject be revealed. Such application shall be directed to the court wherein the trial in which the information is sought is pending. The application shall be granted only if the court after hearing the defendant and the researcher determines that the defendant seeking the information has shown by clear and convincing evidence that:

(1) there is probable cause to believe that the person from whom the information is sought has information which is clearly relevant to the preparation of the defendant's defense;

(2) there is a factual basis for the defendant's need for the information to prepare his defense; and

(3) the same or equivalent information is not available to the defendant from any source other than the researcher.[270]

Researcher Accountability

To Subjects. The need of civil litigants to compel researchers to reveal information cannot readily be generalized. In comparison to criminal adjudication, however, it is rare that the civil litigant will have a constitutional interest in obtaining evidence from the researcher, such as the Sixth Amendment interest of the criminal defendant. Similarly, a civil litigant rarely will have as strong an interest as the state in a criminal proceeding, striving for "fair and effective law enforcement aimed at providing security in person and property of the individual."[271] Hardly ever, therefore, will the interest of a civil litigant in compelling a researcher to reveal information outweigh the First Amendment interest of informing the public served by a researcher's or journalist's privilege.[272] Researcher and journalist privilege statutes, therefore, generally make no broad exceptions for civil litigants.[273]

Proposed[274] and existing[275] journalist privilege statutes, however, do make a specific exception in cases in which a reporter defendant in a libel suit relies on an unidentified source for a defense. This is in response to the U.S. Supreme Court's decisions in New York Times v. Sullivan[276] and its progeny,[277] granting some First Amendment protection for libelous statements in certain circumstances. Under the New York Times standard, a libel plaintiff in these situations must sustain the heavy burden of proving that the statement was made with "actual malice"--that is, with knowledge that it was false or with reckless disregard of whether it was false or not.[278] Subsequently, in St. Amant v. Thompson,[279] the Court made it clear that proof of reckless disregard requires that the plaintiff show "that the defendant, in fact, entertained serious doubts as to the truth of his publication."[280]

Initially, the New York Times standard applied only to the narrow instance in which a public official was seeking recovery for defamatory[281] falsehoods about his or her official behavior. In a series of later decisions, the Court extended the New York Times standard to "public figures," but failed to define the terms "public official" and "public figure" with precision.

The standard enunciated in the New York Times and subsequent cases is difficult for the libel plaintiff to meet.[282] The difficulty is compounded if, in attempting to prove that the defendant entertained serious doubts as to the truth of the publication, the plaintiff is precluded from discovering the unidentified sources and unpublished material on which the defendant may have relied.

While less likely than in the news area, it is possible for a researcher to be a defendant in a libel action. The "public scholar," investigating such subjects as government corruption, foreign policy, industrial mismanagement,[283] and faulty products may be accused of libeling an individual in the course of disseminating to the public[284] the information gathered. Like the journalist, such a researcher would be protected to a degree by the First Amendment as interpreted by the New York Times and subsequent cases. The libel plaintiff will, thus, have to prove willful falsehood or reckless disregard of the truth, a formidable burden. The burden becomes even more difficult if the researcher can, because of the privilege, withhold the source of this information and unpublished material.

It is within the realm of possibility, as well, that researchers communicating information that is not within the New York Times rule will also be defendants in libel actions. The recent California case of White v. State,[285] though not involving a researcher, points out the type of libel action that may be confronted by any individual handling records containing personal data about individuals. The plaintiff had been involved in a "joyriding" incident in 1939; a juvenile record for "grand theft auto" was routinely filed with the California Bureau of Criminal Identification and Investigation (CI&I). Subsequently, in 1941, White was identified, through photographs retained pursuant to his juvenile offense, as a check forger. A notation of this offense was made on White's CI&I file, as well as the facts that White had assumed five aliases and was serving a term in an Oklahoma prison. White, however, was not the check forger. After being rejected for a job as a policeman a number of times over a period of 20 years, the plaintiff finally gained access to his police record and discovered the error. To redress personal damage, White commenced an action against the State of California and the chief of the Bureau of Criminal Identification and Investigation. He asserted two bases of liability: that he was damaged by the defendant's libelous utterances and that he was damaged by the defendant's negligence.

The communication involved in White would not be accorded the First Amendment protection conferred in New York Times v. Sullivan and its progeny. It did, however, fit into a situation in which the libel plaintiff must sustain a heavy burden of proving defendant's malice. White was non-suited on his libel claim because the relevant communication came within a California statute[286] protecting to a degree the dissemination of information at the request of an authorized recipient (the police department). In order to recover damages, actual malice[287] had to be shown. White had made no such allegations.

A libel plaintiff suing a researcher in a non-New York Times v. Sullivan context, thus, because of statutory or common law protection granted to the communication, may be required to sustain a heavier burden than is traditionally required in a libel action. A plaintiff may be required to prove malice.[288] It is difficult to generalize about the types of situations in which communications are granted protection.[289] A number of these are of particular relevance to the research context. The statute invoked in the White case, for example, may pertain to communications made by a researcher, contracted by a government agency to evaluate a particular program, to that government agency. Also, communications between public officers in discharge of official duties are generally at least given this qualified protection.[290] This arguably applies to communications between researchers funded by government agencies and the personnel of the particular agency involved. Furthermore, private citizens are protected in their communications with public authorities relating to such areas as the detection and prevention of crime and the conduct of public officials.[291] Researchers who communicate information about crime or government corruption to government officials are, thus, not subject to the traditional libel standard.

The libel plaintiff suing a researcher who can claim qualified protection from a libel suit, based either on the constitutional interest protected by New York Times v. Sullivan or by a common law or statutory privilege, has a definite interest in discovering the source of the plaintiff's information as well as other unpublished information related to the allegedly libelous statement. A researcher's privilege statute, however, allows the researcher defendant to refuse to disclose the information. The result is that the plaintiff will not be able to meet the burden of proof and the case will be dismissed.

The proposed Statute, however, in the interest of granting as broad a protection as possible, rejects an exception for libel actions. From plaintiffs' point of view, this allows the researcher to be negligent and even untruthful in communicating personal and, perhaps, incriminating information about them without recourse. From the point of view of research activity, it protects the researcher from libel suits aimed only at getting the researcher to reveal sources ("strike suits").[292] The net result of not providing a libel exception, however, is that the plaintiff's extremely difficult burden of proof in these situations is made even more difficult, giving extra license to the researcher's possible negligence and dishonesty in, one hopes, only a small number of cases.

As in the section on criminal defendants, however, a draft for an exception to the privilege for libel actions is provided. The draft is included for two reasons. First, the researcher's privilege Statute is not designed to protect researchers from actions that damage the reputation of their subjects. Secondly, an exception can be drafted whereby the researcher-defendant will only have to reveal the otherwise privileged information upon plaintiff's showing that he or she has a bona fide claim of defamation.[293]

Alternate Provision for a Defamation Exception
Exception for defamation:

(a) The privilege conferred in section 2 of this Act shall not apply in any defamation action where the person seeking disclosure can demonstrate that the identity of the source will lead to relevant evidence on the issue of actual malice.

(b) Notwithstanding the provisions of subdivision 1 of this section, the identity of the source shall not be ordered disclosed unless the following conditions are met:

(1) that there is probable cause to believe that the source has information clearly relevant to the issue of defamation;

(2) the source cannot be obtained by any alternative means.

(c) The court shall make its order on the issue of disclosure after making findings of fact, which order may be appealed to the lowest appellate court. During the appeal the order is stayed and non-disclosure shall remain in full force and effect.[294]

To the Research Community for Reanalysis. The interest of the research community in gaining access to a researcher's data is also potentially in conflict with maintaining confidentiality.[295] The research community may, for example, desire a researcher's data to review and verify the findings of the original project; other researchers may also be interested in reanalyzing the data compiled. To maintain the integrity of the research process, researchers have an obligation to make available their data.

The proposed Statute does not provide for an exception to correspond with the interest of the research community and the corresponding obligation of the researcher. In fact, no researcher privilege statute provides such an exception. The interests of the research community are important and the researcher's obligation to produce the data is real. On balance, however, the interest in maintaining confidentiality is more weighted in terms of both the ethical duty of the researcher to the subject and the interest in informing the public. Furthermore, it is possible for a researcher to devise methods to report data so that it can be used by research communities while still maintaining confidentiality. Raw data can be generally reported without revealing identifying information about subjects.

Federal Statutory Provisions that Conflict with Confidentiality

Two major federal statutes are potentially in conflict with maintaining confidentiality in the context of research done under the auspices of the federal government. They are the Federal Reports Act[296] and the Freedom of Information Act.[297] No attempt to redress this threat to anonymity is specifically made in the proposed statutes. Ideally, however, some accommodation could be provided. Both Acts, though imperfect, foster important interests that have been specifically recognized by Congress. In fact, these interests serve the needs of the researcher to some degree.

The Federal Reports Act. The Federal Reports Act was passed during World War II to eliminate duplication of data gathering endeavors of various arms of the federal government, to maximize the use of data gathered by the federal government, and to minimize the "burden" upon those individuals and businesses required to supply information to the federal government. To achieve these ends, the Reports Act authorizes the Office of Management and Budget[298] to require a federal agency to make information available to another federal agency. This power only exists, however, if one of the following four conditions exist: (1) the information is in the form of statistical summaries; (2) it is not confidential at the time of transfer; (3) the person who supplied the information has given consent to the transfer; (4) the agency receiving the information has mandatory authority to obtain the information on its own.[299]

The Reports Act, therefore, undermines the assurance of confidentiality that a federal researcher privilege statute provides the researcher. With few exceptions, federal researchers may be required to provide the data they collect to federal agencies other than the one for which they work, possibly including law enforcement agencies. Subjects' interest in maintaining privacy and not incriminating themselves or others is, thus, not furthered because of this decrease in confidentiality. Furthermore, federal researchers on ethical grounds may feel that they can only elicit certain types of information if their subjects are informed of and consent to possible release of the data to other agencies. This may be an extremely difficult burden for researchers to meet; they may decide not to pursue certain personal and controversial topics.

The interests furthered by the Federal Reports Act, lessening the burden on individuals who supply the government with information and maximizing the use of information compiled by the government, are in themselves well founded. Furthermore, researchers employed by a federal agency are potential beneficiaries of the Federal Reports Act. They may be able to obtain valuable information with little effort if it has already been compiled by the government. Also, the Federal Reports Act provides a mechanism by which research data compiled by a federal agency is made available for reanalysis with the federal government. As a suggestion, both the interests served by the Federal Reports Act and by a researcher's privilege statute could be better reconciled if either statute included the following two provisions: first, the anonymity provided by the researcher's privilege act be maintained in any federal agency to which the information is transferred; also--and of great importance--the agency to which the information is transferred shall not use the information in a manner that will expose the source of the information to criminal penalties, civil liability, or the termination of government benefits.

The Freedom of Information Act. The Freedom of Information Act was passed in 1966 in response to demands by civil libertarians and the news media to make information maintained by the government available to the public. Secrecy was to be frowned upon and open disclosure fostered.[300]

Unlike the Federal Reports Act, the Freedom of Information Act makes some accommodations to the interest of maintaining confidentiality of certain types of information and protecting the privacy of the individuals who supply the information. Nine exceptions to the disclosure provision are made. Four of these are particularly relevant to protecting information obtained in the course of federal research. They are: (3) matters specifically exempted from disclosure by statute;[301] (4) trade secrets and commercial or financial information obtained from any person and privileged or confidential; (6) personnel and medical files and similar files the disclosure of which would constitute a clearly unwarranted invasion of personal privacy; and (7) investigatory files compiled for law enforcement purposes except to the extent available by law to a private party.

The nine exceptions, however, are not as powerful as the disclosure provision. In the first place, they are not mandatory. The head of an agency can decide to ignore an exception, even if it explicitly applies to the information in question. Also, if the agency decides to withhold information on the basis of an exception, a court can issue an order to disclose. Furthermore, judicial interpretations of these somewhat ambiguous exceptions have not favored the interest of confidentiality. Exemplary of the narrow judicial interpretation of these exceptions is <u>Consumers Union of United States, Inc. v. Veterans Administration</u>.[302] The Consumers Union brought an action to require the Veterans Administration to release the raw scores, scoring scheme, and quality point scores compiled in the VA's testing program of hearing aids. Though the VA had included a policy statement on confidentiality in its request to private manufacturers to supply their hearing aids for the testing program, the court stated that this did not guarantee that the results of the testing, naming the manufacturers, would not be revealed.[303] The fourth exception to the Freedom of Information Act was, therefore, not applicable because the three requirements stated in the statute were not met. The exception applies only when a trade secret is involved, obtained from a person, that is commerical and financial <u>and</u> is privileged and confidential.

Though the Freedom of Information Act attempts to accommodate both the competing interests of disclosure and confidentiality, the confidentiality provisions as interpreted and applied leave much to be desired. Federal researchers, thus, may not be able to resist demands by the public for information they have acquired. Either the subject's privacy is, thus, potentially sacrificed or the researcher must refrain from important research endeavors. The researcher involved in federal evaluation of public benefit programs, for example, may be reluctant to elicit from project beneficiaries personal information that may be crucial to the evaluation endeavor.

The Freedom of Information Act fosters the interest of making governmental information available to the public. This is essential to a democratic society in which the government is ultimately accountable to the public and depends upon an informed citizenry. It is to be emphasized at this point that a researcher privilege statute is designed for the ultimate purpose of providing better information for the public. By assuring anonymity, the statute allows the researcher to pursue controversial and interesting fields of inquiry for the benefit of society. In this sense, the Freedom of Information Act and the proposed Statute are not, as a matter of basic policy, in conflict.

Researchers, whether employed by the federal government or not, are as a class potentially aided by this Act.[304] The government is an important repository of information of value to the researcher.[305] Also, the Act potentially enables non-governmentally affiliated researchers the opportunity to study the policies and workings of the government in fields other than the most sensitive areas of national defense, internal security, and foreign affairs.[306] The Freedom of Information Act, however, could better accommodate the competing interests of confidentiality and informing the public if its exceptions were stated more precisely and were mandatory, rather than at the discretion of the heads of the various agencies and the courts.[307]

PROCEDURAL ISSUES

Who May Invoke the Privilege?

Unlike existing journalist and researcher statutes, the proposed Statute provides that any person can invoke the privilege, whether a researcher or not not.[308] The only prerequisite to invoking the privilege is that the information sought by the subpoena or other legal process be information obtained by a person who comes within the statutory definition of a researcher.[309]

In providing for a privilege for anyone who has access to research data, the Statute attempts to provide the widest possible protection to those individuals who are the subjects of research endeavors. It is recognized that a wide range of individuals potentially have access to research data, including all members of researchers' staffs, reporters, and authors who intend to document the research endeavor, and disinterested third parties who may be present at the time researchers are interviewing subjects. To not protect these individuals would be to provide a potential loophole for agencies that desire to compel testimony relating to the work of a researcher.

Burden of Proving Coverage

No researcher[310] and only one journalist statute[311] specifically sets forth the person who has the burden of proving whether the privilege is applicable to a particular individual.

There are two possibilities for assuming the burden of proof. It can either be required of the party asserting the privilege or of the party requesting the information. If the burden of proof is placed upon the individual asserting the privilege, she or he would have to make a preliminary showing that the information sought is research data as defined in section 5(2) of the proposed Statute. On the other hand, if the burden is placed on the party seeking the information, she or he would have to prove that the information sought is not research data. Failure to sustain this burden would mean that the privilege is automatically effective.

It is obvious that placing the burden of proof on the party seeking the information would make it easier for the individual asserting the privilege to gain protection. This, however, is not the usual way in which privilege conferring statutes generally operate and would require cumbersome specific statutory language. Also, it makes the process for invoking the privilege more complex by requiring one party to invoke the privilege and another to sustain the burden of proof.

The proposed Statute, though drafted to provide maximum protection for the researcher, rejects the placing of the burden of proof on the party requesting the information. By implication the burden of proof is on the individual asserting the privilege. One reason for this is to avoid the two disadvantages pointed out above. The second reason is that the broad coverage of the Statute[312] makes the initial showing to invoke the privilege a very easy one. Thus, placing the burden of proof on the individual asserting the privilege should in no way diminish the effectiveness of the privilege. If the privilege were drafted narrowly, it would be worthwhile to shift the burden of proof to the party requesting the information in order to make it less difficult for the party asserting the privilege.

Procedures in Issuing a Subpoena

A definite means by which the researcher's privilege can be strengthened is to carefully circumscribe the situations in which a subpoena can be issued.

No matter how extensive the substantive protection of the privilege, if a subpoena can be issued only in limited circumstances, the threat to researchers of being compelled to reveal information can be kept to an absolute minimum. Also, law enforcement agencies and other parties seeking information from researchers will be precluded from harassing the researcher by issuing subpoenas. While no existing researcher and journalist privilege statutes contain provisions stipulating pre-subpoena procedures, the journalist privilege bill proposed by Senator Cranston, S-158, contains such a provision. The proposed Statute incorporates nearly verbatim the Cranston bill's section on pre-subpoena procedures.

Section 4 of the proposed Statute sets forth the procedures by which a subpoena may be issued to compel the researcher to testify or produce documents. Section 4(a) specifies the factual burden that must be met by the party requesting the information from the researcher in order for a subpoena to be issued in the first place. The requesting party's burden parallels the qualified journalist's privilege advocated by Justice Stewart in his _Branzburg_[313] dissent. The crucial difference, however, is that the proposed Statute requires that this showing be made before a subpoena is issued. The proposed Statute as well, provides for an "unqualified" privilege if a subpoena is issued. Justice Stewart's proposal, on the other hand, assumes that a subpoena can be issued and directs the privilege itself upon the necessary showing by the requesting party.

Sections 4(b) and 4(c) of the proposed Statute specify the logistics for obtaining a researcher subpoena. Section 4(b) states that, in adjudicative and grand jury proceedings, a court shall determine whether the requesting party has made the proper showing in a subpoena to issue and that, in investigative proceedings, the investigating body shall make the determination. Section 4(c) importantly provides that the hearing conducted by the appropriate body in order to determine if a subpoena shall be issued shall not be an ex parte hearing, attended only by the requesting party. At this early stage, the Statute requires that the researcher be given notice of the hearing as well as an opportunity to be heard. The researcher's testimony thus can be considered by the individual or body conducting the hearing in making its determination. In this way, a researcher will be protected from being served by a subpoena upon a strong showing on his or her part outweighing the testimony of the requesting party. Also, the provision assumes that researchers will be given adequate time to avoid a subpoena if one is eventually issued; they will not be served by a subpoena or other legal process by surprise.

The Statute provides for an appeal of an order issuing or refusing to issue a subpoena or other legal process. In the first place, sections 4(c) and 4(d) of the proposed Statute provide that such an order can be appealed on an interlocutory basis. That is, the order can be appealed before the proceedings go forward. This is particularly advantageous to researchers, for they can appeal the order to issue the subpoena before the subpoena is actually served. They can, thus, potentially prevent the issuance of an improper subpoena before they are actually legally compelled to furnish information and will only have to challenge head-on subpoenas that are judicially sound. It should be noted that whether the decision to issue the subpoena was made by a court or administrative or executive body, the Statute provides that the decision is subject to judicial review. This will assure researchers that there will be uniformity in the requirements for issuing a subpoena whether the issuing agency be a court or non-judicial body. Non-judicial bodies will not be able to issue subpoenas with greater ease than courts.

Finally, the proposed Statute automatically provides that pending an appeal of an order to issue a subpoena, a stay shall be granted prohibiting the issuance of the subpoena. This provision is obviously necessary if an interlocutory appeal is to be meaningful. Such an appeal would be worthless if, during the appeal, the researcher had to answer the contested subpoena or legal process. The statutory provision, however, ensures that the researcher will not have to be identified with providing the necessary showing of irreparable harm in order for a stay of the proceedings to be issued.

WAIVER

Introduction

In the context of a privilege against compelled disclosure, waiver can be viewed as the power to divest the privilege by voluntarily disclosing privileged information. Despite the apparent simplicity of this definition, waiver is a complex issue facing the drafter of a privilege conferring statute. First, it must be decided if an explicit provision for waiver will be included in the statute. If the choice is made to include a waiver provision, serious consideration must be given to the purpose of the privilege, who the privilege is designed to benefit, and who controls the privilege.

The preliminary inquiry is whether an explicit provision for waiver should be included in the proposed Statute. At least one researcher privilege statute[314] and a few journalist statutes[315] provide explicit waiver provisions. In the absence of waiver provision in journalist statutes, a number of courts have held that voluntary disclosure of a source of information precludes a reporter from asserting a privilege. The experience of reporters, claiming a privilege under the New York privilege statute[316] that does not contain a waiver provision, points this out. In People v. Wolf,[317] the court denied a motion by the Village Voice to quash a subpoena duces tecum to produce the manuscript of an article concerning confessions of inmates participating in a prison riot at the New York "Tombs." The court reasoned that because the Voice had published the article under the by-line of an inmate, it had waived the privilege conferred by the New York statute.

In re Dan,[318] a more recent case, provided a similar result. The state attorney general moved to compel a reporter and photographer to testify as to what they had observed during the prison disturbance at Attica before a grand jury investigating the incident. Inasmuch as one of the witnesses had already made a statement to the attorney general regarding his observations, the privilege was deemed waived and the witnesses could be compelled to testify despite the New York statute.

Because courts may effectively read a waiver provision into privilege statutes that do not contain them,[319] the proposed Statute includes an explicit waiver provision.[320] By including a narrowly drawn waiver provision, courts will be restricted from possibly flaunting the purpose of the statutory protection by implying waiver in inappropriate situations.

Who May Waive the Privilege?

The party or parties who have the power to waive a privilege in essence control the privilege. They decide whether the privilege will remain in effect. The professional privileges are only waivable by the confider, not the confidant. For example, the attorney-client privilege can be waived only by the client[321] and the doctor-patient privilege only by the patient.[322] On the other hand, those few journalist statutes that include waiver provisions make the privilege waivable only by the journalist or confidant and not by the source or confider.[323]

Because the power to waive the privilege is in essence control of the privilege, the party or parties whom the privilege is designed to protect should have the power of waiver. If the party agrees to disclose the information, there is no further reason to grant the privilege. In the case of the professional privileges, it is clear that their raison d'etre is to allow the individual seeking professional services to be candid and open with the professional. On the other hand, the researcher's privilege is ultimately designed to further the social interest of informing the public.

The proposed Statute is unique in requiring that both the confider and confidant waive the privilege in certain circumstances. The protection provided by the privilege focuses upon guaranteeing that the identity and certain information supplied by the subject be confidential,[324] allowing for investigations in varied and controversial areas. The subject will be more willing to be candid about revealing personal and controversial, sometimes incriminating, information. The researcher will be less reluctant to employ techniques such as field observations that may well reveal personal, controversial, and sometimes incriminating information about subjects. The ethical transgressions involved in observational techniques that often invade the subject's privacy are somewhat offset by the fact that the researcher cannot be compelled to divulge the subject's identity and information obtained. The statute, thus, should provide that the subject must consent before the privilege is waived.

While the research subject has the greatest personal stake of all interested parties in the protection granted by the privilege, the researcher's personal interest is substantial. The researcher is concerned that the results of research work will not be revealed prematurely. Tentative preliminary results may be misleading. Their exposure may result in the termination of the project, for they may suggest that the investigation is not yielding results that are favorable to the sponsor. This would sacrifice the objectivity and academic integrity to which researchers are theoretically dedicated. Also, premature exposure of results may prejudice the responses of further subjects that are required to finalize the project. The proposed Statute, therefore, provides that, in addition to the subject, the researcher has a say commensurate with her or his interest in determining whether the privilege is waived.[325]

To reflect the prime interest of the subject in the Statute's protection, the waiver provision provides that under all conditions the subject must consent before the privilege is deemed waived. The researcher's consent is needed for waiver of the privilege only when the researcher is called upon to disclose information that the Statute protects. If the subject is subpoenaed to reveal information protected by the Statute and does so, the privilege is waived without the researcher's consent. The net effect of this waiver scheme is that the subject can waive the privilege by personally disclosing information protected by the Statute. If, however, the researcher is subpoenaed or otherwise compelled to reveal information protected by the Statute, the subject's consent to waiving the privilege will not dissolve the Statute's protection. The researcher must, also, so consent. On the other hand, in this situation, the researcher's consent to waive the privilege only is effective if the subject concurs.

Because the Statute's protection extends beyond the identity of the subject and operates even when no express or implied promise of confidentiality is made, a problem may arise in the situation where the researcher is compelled to disclose information relating to anonymous subjects.[326] Under such circumstances it is impossible for the subject to waive the privilege. The Statute thus provides that researchers, alone, can waive the privilege upon a showing that they do not have knowledge of the subject's identity.[327] This provision will not seriously infringe upon the protection that the Statute provides for the subject, for without knowledge of the subject's identity, it is difficult for the information revealed to be used to the detriment of the subject by the subpoenaing agency.

When is Waiver Effective?

The proposed Statute provides that voluntary disclosure of privileged information operates as a waiver only when the party (or parties) empowered to waive the privilege supplies the information in response to a subpoena or other legal process. Any other disclosure of the information does not result in the dissolution of the privilege. Thus, if the researcher publishes or disseminates to the public information that is otherwise privileged, he or she still may assert the privilege to resist a subsequent subpoena or legal process.[328] This type of provision is necessary to further ensure that information obtained in the course of research that is potentially detrimental to the subject not be readily available to governmental agencies. This helps foster an overriding concern of the Statute--to make personal and controversial information available for the use of researchers. Further, if the privilege is waived, it is waived only as to the information disclosed at the time of the waiver. The door is not opened to compelled disclosure of information that has not been revealed in accordance with the waiver provision. The parties empowered to waive the privilege are, thus, in total control of the extent of the waiver.

Presence of a Third Party

Unlike the professional privileges,[329] the privilege conferred by the proposed Statute is not divested if a "casual disinterested third party" is present at the time of the privileged communication. There are a number of reasons for not conforming to this general practice among professional privileges. The professional privileges are conferred solely to confidential communications. Logically, the presence of a disinterested third party would destroy confidentiality at the onset. The researcher's privilege as provided in the proposed statute, however, is not based on confidentiality. In addition, the professional privileges protect only information revealed in the course of a direct conversation between the professional and the client. The researcher's privilege protects information obtained by the researcher employing techniques that involve methods other than direct communication. For example, the proposed Statute protects information obtained in the course of observing the actions of subjects as well as observing the conversations between subjects and not including the researcher. If the privilege were automatically waived when a third disinterested party was present, the protection given in the mentioned situations would be meaningless.

Procedures for Waiving the Privilege

The less complicated context in which the privilege may be waived is when the subject is compelled to testify as to information that is privileged under the proposed Statute. The mere compliance with the subpoena or other legal process will constitute a waiver of the privilege, for the subject alone can waive the privilege if called to testify.

When the researcher is compelled to testify as to privileged information, a waiver may only be accomplished by the consent of both the researcher and the subject. The proposed Statute puts the burden of obtaining the subject's consent to a waiver on the researcher. The researcher must either produce a written statement signed by the subject or the subject's agent, authorizing the waiver, or the researcher must provide for a personal appearance of the subject.

Whether the subject waives the privilege in complying with the subpoena or consents to the researcher waiving the privilege, the proposed Statute provides that the subject must attest to the fact that she or he has "knowingly and voluntarily" waived the privilege. This will help ensure that subjects have not been coerced to waive the privilege and that they know the consequences of their release of the information. This requirement is also made in the case where the researcher's consent is needed to waive the privilege for similar reasons.

REFERENCES AND NOTES

1. For an extended and detailed discussion of the interests of these parties at interest see Nejelski and Lerman, A Researcher-Subject Testimonial Privilege: What to Do Before the Subpoena Arrives, 1971 WIS. L. REV. 1085-93 (1971) [hereinafter cited as NEJELSKI and LERMAN]. See also Nejelski and Finsterbusch, The Prosecutor and the Researcher: Present and Prospective Variations of the Supreme Court's Branzburg Decision, 21 SOC. PROBS. 3 (1973) [hereinafter cited as NEJELSKI and FINSTERBUSCH].
2. All levels (federal, state, and local) and all branches (executive, legislative, and judicial and their agencies) of government.
3. The Press Censorship Newsletter No. V, Aug.-Sept., 1974, lists 29 judicial, legislative, or executive agency problems concerning the protection of confidential sources and information.
4. 418 U.S. 683 (1974).
5. Letter from Dr. Wadell Pomeroy to Paul Nejelski and Lindsey Lerman, Feb. 6, 1971, reported in NEJELSKI and LERMAN, supra note 1 at 1090 n. 17.
6. A. Kinsey, W. Pomeroy, and A. Martin, SEXUAL BEHAVIOR IN THE HUMAN MALE 47 (1948).
7. Kershaw and Small, Data Confidentiality and Privacy: Lessons from the New Jersey Negative Income Tax Experiment, 20 PUB. POLICY 257 (1972).
8. See Advisory Committee for ACE Study on Campus Unrest, Statement on Confidentiality, Use of Results and Independence, 165 SCIENCE 158, 159 (1969).
9. United States v. Doe (Appeal of Samuel L. Popkin), 460 F. 2d 328 (1st Cir. 1972), cert. denied, Popkin v. U.S. 411 U.S. 909 (1973).
10. Such a privilege does not extend to communications between scholars.
11. 460 F. 2d at 333.
12. United States v. Doe (In the Matter of a Grand Jury Subpoena Served upon Richard Falk), 332 F. Supp. 938 (D. Mass. 1971).
13. United States v. Doe (In the Matter of a Grand Jury Subpoena Served upon Leonard Rodberg), 332 F. Supp. 930 (D. Mass. 1971), modified 455 F. 2d 753 (1st Cir. 1972), modified sub nom., Gravel v. United States, 408 U.S. 606 (1972).
14. U.S. CONST. art. I., sec. 6, I. 1 " . . . for any Speech or Debate in either House, they [Senators and Representatives] shall not be questioned in any other Place."

15. 408 U.S. at 625-26.
16. Fisher v. Citizens' Committee, 72 Misc. 2d 595, 339 N.Y.S. 2d 853 (Sup. Ct. 1973).
17. Discussed in People v. Newman, 32 N.Y. 2d 379, 298 N.E. 2d 651, 345 N.Y.S. 2d 502 (1973), cert. denied, 414 U.S. 1163 (1974).
18. Contained in a letter to Hon. Robert W. Kastenmeier from Otto Larsen, Executive Officer of the ASA, reported in Hearings on Newsmen's Privilege Before Subcomm. No. 3 of the House Comm. on the Judiciary, 93rd Cong., 1st Sess. at 540 (1973). The letter further stated: "While Professor Popkin has been released from jail, the problem persists; and in every scholarly community, there is mounting pressure over the issues and uncertainties posed by recent court action."
19. V. Blasi, Press Subpoenas: An Empirical and Legal Analysis, 70 MICH. L. REV. 229 (1971) [hereinafter referred to as BLASI REPORT].
20. Id. at 247.
21. Nejelski, Researchers in West German Survey Report Difficulty in Obtaining or Protecting Confidential Data, 1 ASA FOOTNOTES at 2 (1973).
22. 408 U.S. 665 (1972). In Branzburg, the Court considered three situations in which reporters were subpoenaed to grand juries to disclose information they gathered in the course of their investigations. All three reporters asserted that the First Amendment protected them from such disclosure. Paul Branzburg of the Carrier-Journal in Louisville, Kentucky, was subpoenaed to identify individuals who were the subject of his article on the manufacture of drugs and narcotics. Paul Pappas, a television newsman and photographer, was allowed to remain in Black Panther headquarters in New Bedford, Massachusetts, to report on the events of an anticipated police raid. The raid never took place, but Pappas was subpoenaed to testify as to the events that occurred while in the Panther headquarters. Earl Caldwell, a black reporter for The New York Times, was subpoenaed to testify as to certain information he had obtained in the course of the confidential relationship he had developed with the Black Panthers. For a detailed discussion of the effect of Branzburg in the researcher area, see NEJELSKI and FINSTERBUSCH, supra note 1.
23. 408 U.S. at 704, quoting with approval Lovell v. Griffin, 303 U.S. 444, 450 (1938).
24. 408 U.S. at 705. Similarly, two pre-Branzburg lower federal court decisions defined "press" broadly. United States v. Doe (In the Matter of a Grand Jury Subpoena Served upon Richard Falk), 332 F. Supp. 938 (D. Mass. 1971), defined the public interest served by the First Amendment to be "the maximization of the spectrum of available knowledge," including newspapers and information available in books and articles. Accord, United States v. Doe (Appeal of Samuel L. Popkin), supra note 9, identifying a First Amendment interest in the "continued flow of information to scholars about public problems."
25. See "Coverage: People" at B-31ff, infra for a discussion of First Amendment protection as it extends to researchers only to the extent to which their work is publicly beneficial.
26. 408 U.S. at 690.
27. Id. at 690-91.
28. Id. at 700.

29. 470 F. 2d 778 (2d Cir. 1972).
30. 356 F. Supp. 1394 (D.D.C. 1973).
31. Id. at 1398-99.
32. 354 F. Supp. 208 (D.D.C. 1972).
33. 408 U.S. at 699-700.
34. Costello v. United States, 350 U.S. 359 (1956).
35. DeGregory v. Attorney General of New Hampshire, 383 U.S. 825, 829 (1966).
36. NAACP v. Alabama, 357 U.S. 449 (1958).
37. 408 U.S. at 707-08. The Court continued by stating that motions to quash subpoenas provide judicial control of grand juries, which are subject to both First and Fifth Amendment limitations. Id. at 708.
38. 408 U.S. at 710.
39. The minority was split as to the type of privilege mandated by the First Amendment. Justices Stewart, Brennan, and Marshall agreed that the government could be compelled to reveal confidences to the grand jury if the government could: "(1) show that there is probable cause to believe that the newsman has information which is clearly relevant to a specific probable violation of law; (2) demonstrate that the information sought cannot be obtained by an alternative means less destructive of First Amendment Rights; and (3) demonstrate a compelling and overriding interest in the information." Id. at 743. Douglas, however, called for an absolute privilege.
40. See, e.g., Baker v. F & F Investment, 470 F. 2d at 785 (public interest in compelled disclosure will often be weightier than the private interest in compelled disclosure); Democratic National Committee v. McCord, 350 F. Supp. at 1397, (Court viewed the interest in maintaining an informed public on the developments of the Watergate incident, involving corruption in the highest circles of government and in the campaign for the presidency, to outweigh the interests of private litigants in compelling reporters to reveal information).
41. Bridge v. New Jersey, 120 N.J. Super. 460, 295 A. 2d 3 (1972), cert. denied, 410 U.S. 911 (1973).
42. Hearings on Newsmen's Privilege Before Subcomm. No. 3 of the House Comm. on the Judiciary, 92nd Cong., 2nd Sess. at 220 (1972).
43. Lightman v. Maryland, 266 Md. 550, 295 A. 2d 212 (1972), cert. denied, 411 U.S. 951 (1973).
44. See House Hearings, supra note 42 at 249. See also, Hearings on Newsmen's Privilege Before Subcomm. on Constitutional Rights of the Senate Comm. on the Judiciary, 93rd Cong., 1st Sess. (1973) (testimony of Joseph Weiler).
45. See Senate Hearings, supra note 44 at 242-43.
46. In re Nowakowki, U.S. District Court for the Eastern District of Wisconsin, No. 72-C-534, order stayed, U.S. Court of Appeals for the Seventh Circuit, No. 72-1845.
47. Los Angeles Times, December 20, 1972.
48. Tennessee v. Thornton, Hamilton County Criminal Court Proceedings, No. 124544, order stayed, Tennessee Court of Civil Appeals, No. 368 (1972).
49. United States v. Liddy, 478 F. 2d 586 (D.C. Cir. 1972).
50. See, e.g., House Hearings, supra note 42 at 211 (testimony of William J. Small, Vice President of C.B.S. News).

51. Subsequent sections will focus upon other aspects of existing and proposed statutes, such as scope of protection, types of information protected, etc.
52. N.Y. CIVIL RIGHTS LAW § 79-j (McKinney Supp. 1972).
53. MD. CODE ANN. art. 35 § 101 (1971).
54. E.g., the State Board of Health and Mental Hygiene is specifically authorized to undertake drug research (MD. CODE ANN. art. 43 § 1-I (1971)).
55. PUB. L. 91-513, 84 Stat. 1236 (1970).
56. 42 U.S.C. § 242a(a)(2) (1970).
57. 21 U.S.C. § 872(c) (1970).
58. H.R. Rep. No. 1444, 91st Cong., 2d Sess. 28 (1970).
59. The Secretary of Health, Education, and Welfare has promulgated regulations that automatically grant the privilege to methadone researchers.
60. Phone conversation with Harold Murray, General Counsel's Office, Bureau of Narcotics and Dangerous Drugs, on June 25, 1973.
61. PUB. L. 91-616, 84 Stat. 1848 (1970).
62. 42 U.S.C. § 4582 (1971).
63. See People v. Newman, supra note 17, for a discussion that the 1972 Act is complementary to the 1970 Act and does not supercede the 1970 Act's wider and more complete coverage.
64. PUB. L. 92-255, 86 Stat. 979 (1972).
65. 21 U.S.C. § 1175(a) (Supp. 1972).
66. 21 U.S.C. § 1103(b) (Supp. 1972).
67. See generally FED. RULES OF EVIDENCE 5.
68. 13 U.S.C. § 9 (1971).
69. See U.S. CONST. art. I, sec. 2, cl. 3.
70. 42 U.S.C. § 1306 (1970).
71. 408 U.S. 665 (1972).
72. E.g., N.Y. CIVIL RIGHTS LAW § 79-h(b) (McKinney 1970) extending coverage only to professional journalists--"one who, for gain or livelihood is engaged in gathering, preparing, or editing of news for a newspaper, magazine, news agency, press association or wire service" [emphasis added]--§ 79-h(a)(6) and newscasters--"a person who for gain or livelihood is engaged in analyzing, commenting on a broadcasting, news by radio or television transmission" [emphasis added]--§ 79-h(a)(7). Note that a "newspaper" must be printed and distributed not less than once a week and qualify for second class mailing in a U.S. post office, § 79-h(a)(1).
73. E.g., H.R. DOC. NO. 3975, 93rd Cong., 1st Sess. § 5 (1973) extends protection to "legitimate members of the professional news media," defined as a "bona fide newsman, such as an individual regularly engaged in earning his or her principal income, or regularly engaged as a principal vocation" in publishing or transmitting matters of public welfare.
74. Hearings on Freedom of the Press Before Subcomm. on Constitutional Rights of the House Comm. on the Judiciary, 92nd Cong., 1st and 2d Sess. 68, 69 (1972).
75. 408 U.S. at 705.
76. Falk argued that "a quite common and natural occurrence is the welding of journalistic activities with scholarly pursuits" in claiming protection under the Court of Appeals decision in U.S. v. Caldwell, 434 F. 2d 1081 (9th Cir. 1970), rev'd, 408 U.S. 665 (1972). Brief on motion to quash subpoena, U.S. v. Doe (D. Mass.) No. 71-165, Sept. 7, 1971.

77. ALAS. COMP. LAWS ANN. § 09.25.150 (Supp. 1970).
78. ARK. STAT. ANN. § 43-917 (1964).
79. Adopted in the 1973 session of the Minnesota legislature.
80. § 3 of the Minnesota Act.
81. H.R. DOC. NO. 3482, 93rd Cong., 1st Sess. § 4 (1973).
82. "Journalist" is defined as anyone who is or has been engaged in gathering, preparing, editing, analyzing, commenting on, writing, broadcasting, or processing information for a newspaper, magazine, radio station, television station, book or wire or news service, and any employee or agent thereof." H.R. DOC. NO. 3482, 93d Cong., 1st Sess. § 5(8) (1973).
83. "News media" is defined as "any newspaper, magazine or other periodical, radio station, television station, book or pamphlet, or wire or news service, any employee or agent thereof, and any individual, partnership, corporation or other legal entity owning, publishing or operating the same." H.R. DOC. NO. 3482, 93rd Cong., 1st Sess. § 5(7) (1973).
84. S. DOC. NO. 158, 93d Cong., 1st Sess. (1973).
85. This discussion will not be concerned with defensive research designs that have been developed to preserve confidentiality of research data. See, e.g., Robert Boruch, <u>Strategies for Eliciting and Merging Confidential Data</u>, 3 POLICY SCIENCES 275 (1972) for discussion of the elaborate "link system" designed to maintain confidentiality in longitudinal studies.
86. E.g., American Anthropological Association, American Psychological Association, American Sociological Association.
87. E.g., Code of Ethics of the American Sociological Association:
>   Confidential information provided by a research
>   subject must be treated as such by the sociologist.
>   Even though research information is not a privileged
>   communication, under the law, the sociologist must
>   as far as possible protect subjects and informants.

    Compare this rather weak policy statement of the American Sociological Association with the strong statement on confidentiality of the American Newspaper Guild quoted infra note 88.
88. The American Newspaper Guild states: "Newspapermen shall refuse to reveal confidences or disclose sources of confidential information in court or before other judicial or investigative bodies." Quoted with approval in Justice Stewart's dissent in <u>Branzburg</u>. 408 U.S. at 732.
89. Advisory Committee for ACE Study on Campus Unrest, supra note 8.
90. <u>Note, Social Research and Privileged Data</u>, 4 VALPARAISO U. L. REV. 368, 396 (1970).
91. 8 Wigmore, EVIDENCE § 2377 at 780.
92. 3 U.S.C. § 301 (1971):
>   The head of an executive department may prescribe regulations for the government of his
>   department, the conduct of its employees, the
>   distribution and performance of its business,
>   and the custody, use, and preservation of its
>   records, papers, and property. This section
>   does not authorize withholding information from
>   the public or limiting the availability of
>   records to the public.

93. 4 VALPARAISO U. L. REV. at 397.
94. Id.
95. NEJELSKI and LERMAN, supra note 1 at 1102 n. 54.
96. 5 U.S.C. § 552 (1971).
97. Address of Attorney General Mitchell before the House of Delegates of the ABA, Aug. 10, 1971, reported in N.Y. Times, April 11, 1970, at 24, col. 1. See NEJELSKI and LERMAN, supra note 1 at 1106 n. 65a for an adaptation of the Justice Department standards to the researcher-subject context.
98. An extension of the Prosecutorial Guidelines for Issuing Press Subpoenas that would include researchers has been proposed to the Department of Justice and is under consideration at this time.
99. 408 U.S. at 706-07.
100. See "Case Histories" at B-12ff. supra.
101. E.g., attorney-client, physician-patient, psychotherapist-patient.
102. E.g., 13 U.S.C. § 9 (1971), prohibiting official disclosure of census information and granting a privileged status to census reports; 42 U.S.C. § 2240 (1971), making inadmissible in evidence in actions for damages required reports of nuclear facility licenses; 42 U.S.C. § 242a(a) (1971) and 21 U.S.C. § 872(c) (1971), conferring upon the Secretary of Health, Education, and Welfare and the Attorney General discretion to grant a testimonial privilege to individuals involved in drug research; 42 U.S.C. § 4582 (1971), conferring upon the Secretary of Health, Education, and Welfare discretion to grant a testimonial privilege to individuals involved in research in alcoholism. Note, however, that Congress is presently considering the passage of a broad privilege law for journalists.
103. See note 101 supra.
104. The proposed Federal Rules of Evidence include the following privileges: required reports privilege (§ 502); lawyer-client privilege (§ 503); psychotherapist-patient privilege (§ 504); and husband-wife privilege (§ 505). The enactment of the proposed Rules as they presently stand has been postponed by Congress' decision to further consider them. The Rules of Evidence are not statutory but are promulgated by the Supreme Court.
105. The decision to rely on federal common law or on the privilege rules in effect in the state in which the federal court is sitting is a complex issue of federal procedure. See generally 34 L.Ed. 2d No. 5, 37, 38, Advisory Committee's Notes on the Federal Rules of Evidence, Art. V. Privileges. The Notes point out that federal common law has been most firmly established as the basis for applying general privileges in federal criminal cases. See FED. R. CRIM. P. 26 (1973). In cases involving federal questions, it is clear that federal privilege law applies, yet the preponderance of the circuit courts have held the state privilege laws inapplicable. See, e.g., In re Lindley Lee Memorial Hospital, 209 F. 2d 122 (2d Cir. 1953), cert. denied, 347 U.S. 960 (1954) (doctor-patient privilege); United States v. Brunner, 200 F. 2d 276 (6th Cir. 1952) (husband-wife privilege). Contra, Baird v. Koevner, 279 F. 2d 623 (9th Cir. 1960) (attorney-client privilege). Finally, in diversity cases where state law generally applies if it is "outcome determinative," Hanna v. Plummer, 380 U.S. 460 (1965), has been interpreted to mean that the decision as to whether state or federal privilege law applies is one of choice rather than constitutional necessity.

106. E.g., the researchers involved in the study and effect of the federal negative income tax experiment in New Jersey had to deal with the threat of compulsory process by both state and federal prosecutors. See "Case Histories" at B-12ff. supra. As in the case of the negative income tax evaluation, state and federal agencies may often be concerned with exactly the same issue such as investigating particular criminal activity.
107. See "Current Judicial Protection" at B-16ff. supra. A possible limitation to First Amendment protection of researchers may be that the protection extends only to those researchers who either communicate the fruits of their work to the public or who will do so in the foreseeable future.
108. "Nor is it suggested that news gathering does not qualify for First Amendment protection; without some protection for seeking out the news, freedom of the press would be eviscerated." 408 U.S. at 681.
109. Id. at 690. This is because the Court's holding was premised solely on the records presently before it, which in the Court's opinion showed "a consequential, yet uncertain burden on news gathering." Also, the Court stated that "Congress has the freedom to determine whether a statutory newsman's privilege is necessary and desirable and to fashion standards and rules as narrow or as broad as deemed necessary to deal with the evil discerned . . ." Id. at 706.
110. "The Congress shall have the power to enforce, by appropriate legislation, the provisions of this article."
111. 384 U.S. 641 (1966).
112. 384 U.S. at 651.
113. Section 5 of the Fourteenth Amendment has been interpreted to have the same broad scope as the Necessary and Proper Clause of the Constitution, U.S. CONST. art. 1, sec. 8, cl. 18. 384 U.S. at 651. The scope of this Clause was described by Chief Justice Marshall in McCulloch v. Maryland, 17 U.S. (4 Wheat.) 157, 206 (1819):

> Let the end be legitimate, let it be within the scope
> of the Constitution, and all means which are appro-
> priate, which are plainly adopted to that end, which
> are not prohibited, but consist with the letter and
> spirit of the Constitution, are constitutional.

But see Oregon v. Mitchell, 400 U.S. 112 (1970), which indicates that the power of Congress to implement the Fourteenth Amendment is not unlimited. See, e.g., Opinion of Justice Black suggesting that the implementation of the Equal Protection Clause through Section 5 of the Fourteenth Amendment should be limited to legislation related to redress racial discrimination and, thus, not extend to a statute which lowers the voting age in state and local elections. Id. at 130.

114.
> Whatever legislation is appropriate, that is adapted
> to carry out the objects the amendments have in view,
> whatever tends to enforce submission to the prohibi-
> tion they contain, and to secure to all persons the
> enjoyment of perfect equality of civil rights and
> equal protection of the laws against State denial or
> or invasion, if not prohibited is brought within
> the domain of congressional power.

Ex Parte Virginia, 100 U.S. 339, 345-46 (1879).

115. § 4(1) of the Voting Rights Act of 1971, providing that persons who successfully completed the sixth grade in a public or private school in Puerto Rico in which the language of instruction is other than English shall not be denied the right to vote because of inability to read or write English. 384 U.S. at 643.

116. The Court rejected New York State's argument that congressional power pursuant to Section 5 of the Fourteenth Amendment can only be sustained if the state law that the congressional statute was designed to displace is judicially held to violate the Equal Protection Clause of the Fourteenth Amendment. Section 5 of the Fourteenth Amendment has enlarged the power of Congress. 384 U.S. at 648. The Court, thus, viewed its decision in Lassiter v. Northampton Election Board, 360 U.S. 45 (1959), sustaining an English literacy requirement, similar to that which § 4(1) of the Voting Rights Act of 1971 displaces, as "an opposite." Id. at 649.

117. See, e.g., Edwards v. California, 372 U.S. 229, 235 (1963); Bantam Books, Inc. v. Sullivan, 372 U.S. 58, 72 (1963).

118. For support of this position in the journalist area, see, e.g., Committee on Federal Legislation, Committee Report: Journalists' Privilege Legislation, 28 THE RECORD 308, 312-14 (1973), and see Senate Hearings, supra note 44 (testimony of Anthony Amsterdam). Contra, House Hearings, supra note 42 at 91 (testimony of Roger C. Cramton).

119. U.S. CONST. art. I, sec. 8, cl. 3.

120. See Gibbons v. Ogden, 22 U.S. (9 Wheat.) 1, 196 (1824); Wickard v. Filburn, 317 U.S. 111 (1942).

121. The Supremacy Clause, U.S. CONST. art. IV, cl. 2.

122. U.S. CONST. art. I, sec. 8, cl. 18.

123. E.g., regulation of lotteries (Lottery Case, 188 U.S. 321 (1903)); drug labeling (Weeks v. United States, 245 U.S. 294 (1964)); and loan shark activities (Perez v. United States, 402 U.S. 146 (1971)).

124. The Communications Act of 1934, 48 Stat. 1081, requiring federal licensing of radio and television stations is constitutionally based on the assumption that all public broadcasting is engaged in or affects interstate commerce, 47 U.S.C. § 301 (1971).

125. The Newspaper Preservation Act of 1970, 84 Stat. 466, exempts certain activities of local newspapers from federal anti-trust laws that pertain only to activities in interstate commerce, 15 U.S.C. § 1801 (1971).

126. If local newspapers are held to be "in" or to "affect" interstate commerce because, for example, they have a connection with national wire services, books, magazines, and journals that are clearly circulated throughout the nation, they can be viewed as within commerce. Note that following this reasoning, a shield law for journalists can readily be justified by the Commerce Clause. See sources cited in note 118 supra for authorities supporting and rejecting the commerce rationale for a privilege statute for journalists.

127. Most researchers will disseminate information both on a face-to-face basis and in journals, books, periodicals, etc. The interrelation between these two methods of dissemination of research data could conceivably be viewed by Congress as "affecting" commerce and, thus, be subject to Commerce Clause regulations. The Supreme Court has allowed wide discretion for Congress to make such a finding. See Wickard v. Filburn, 317 U.S.

111 (1942), which held that pursuant to the Commerce Clause the production of home grown wheat could be regulated. "The effect of consumption of home-grown wheat on interstate commerce is due to the fact that it constitutes the most variable factor in the disappearance of the wheat crop." Id. at 127.

128. U.S. CONST. art. I, sec. 8, cl. 18. An example of the exercise of the Necessary and Proper Clause is the promulgation of housekeeping statutes allowing federal agencies to administer and enforce acts of Congress. See, e.g., § 104(a) of the Immigration and Naturalization Act, 8 U.S.C. § 1104(a) (1971).

129. See, e.g., 21 U.S.C. § 872(c) (1971) and 42 U.S.C. § 242(a) (1971) (confidentiality provisions of the Comprehensive Drug Abuse Prevention and Control Act of 1970); 42 U.S.C. § 4582 (1971) (confidentiality provision of the Comprehensive Alcohol and Alcoholism Prevention, Treatment, and Rehabilitation Act of 1970).

130. The general power of the heads of federal agencies to enter into contracts and award grants for basic science research to institutions of higher learning or non-profit organizations whose primary purpose is the conducting of scientific research is conferred by 42 U.S.C. § 1891 (1970). See Grossbaum, Grants for Scientific Research: Reassessment of a Counter Productive Statute, 30 FED. B.J. 181 (1970) for a discussion that "basic scientific research" includes the social sciences. More specific examples of statutes authorizing research commissioned by federal agencies include a statute empowering the Small Business Administration to make grants to state agencies, universities, and to state-charted development, audit, and finance corporations to research, study, and compile statistical data to help provide technical and managerial aids for small businesses, 15 U.S.C. 636(d) (1971). Funds may also be used to make grants to state or local agencies for research on mass transportation, 49 U.S.C. § 1607(b) (Supp. 1972). Also, the Director of OEO is empowered to "contract or make other arrangements for independent evaluations" of programs authorized under the Economic Opportunity Act, 42 U.S.C. 2995(a) (Supp. 1973).

131. See, e.g., Simkins v. Moses H. Cone Memorial Hospital, 323 F. 2d 959 (4th Cir. 1963). The court viewed the allocation of massive federal funds through state agencies to private hospitals to be the most important factor in rendering the private hospitals' activities "state action" and therefore subject to the requirements of the Fourteenth Amendment. Id. at 967. But see City of Boston v. Volpe, 464 F. 2d 254 (1st Cir. 1972) in which the court stated that federal funding does not render a project "forever federal." Federal funding can be provided for preliminary studies, for example, followed by complete federal abstention and purely state or local support. Id. at 258.

132. See, e.g., Silva v. Romney, 473 F. 2d 287 (1st Cir. 1973), in which the court noted the important goal of providing adequate housing for low and moderate income families as a significant factor in deciding that the allocation of HUD funds to provide mortgage guarantees and interest grants to private developers rendered the project "federal." Id. at 292.

133. See, e.g., Silva v. Romney, supra note 132 where, the court considered the important federal goal of protecting the environment in sustaining federal regulation of the environmental features of the HUD-assisted private housing development; Simkins v. Moses H. Cone Memorial Hospital,

B-71

supra note 131, in which the court considered the consequences of allowing a hospital to escape the anti-discrimination requirements of the Fourteenth Amendment if state action was not found. 323 F. 2d at 967.

134. E.g., Citta v. Delaware Valley Hospital, 313 F. Supp. 301, 307 (E.D. Pa. 1970) in which the court stated that absent massive or substantial input of federal funds, federal court jurisdiction under the state action doctrine may still be maintained because the receipt of Hill-Burton hospital funds from the federal government obligates the state to maintain "a fair and just governance of the hospitals receiving the aid." Id. at 307.

135. Rieken, The Federal Government and Social Science Policy, 394 ANNALS 100, 102 (1971).

136. See La Raza Unida v. Volpe, 337 F. Supp. 221 (N.D. Calif. 1971) which held that federal restrictions concerning population displacement and environmental considerations attach to a "federal-aid" highway project upon location and approval of the highway system. The authorization of approval of federal funds for the project was unnecessary. The court's holding was largely based on two factors: one was the language of the Uniform Relocation Act and relevant regulations, which on their face showed how the welfare money was to be allocated; second and significantly was the existence of the strong federal policies relating to the problems of highway displacement and environmental protection. Id. at 229.

137. 42 U.S.C. 242a(a) (1971).

138. 21 U.S.C. 872(a) (1970).

139. H.R. REP., No. 1444, supra note 58.

140. See Florida Lime and Avocado Growers Inc. v. Paul, 373 U.S. 132 (1963), in which the court stated that federal regulation of agricultural commodities by minimum standards, rather than a design to preempt the field for purposes of marketing regulation, did not displace the state's authority to require more stringent standards to serve the interest of consumers within the state.

141. See Campbell v. Hussey, 368 U.S. 297 (1961), in which the Court held that the Federal Tobacco Inspection Act preempted the field and made supplemented state regulation invalid.

142. Unlike individuals who are members of professions that require licensing (such as law and medicine) and who are thus readily identifiable, researchers are truly an amorphous group of individuals who are not generally licensed and who are not represented by a single professional organization. Cf. Branzburg v. Hayes, 408 U.S. 665 (1972) in which the Court noted the difficulty in defining who is a newsman. Id. at 704.

143. See 408 U.S. at 688 and note 168 infra. The Branzburg Court noted that the public generally has a right to everyone's evidence. Consequently, any exception to the general rule should be carefully limited to the intended group.

144. Hanson, An Analysis of State Newsman Privilege: Legislation and Cases Arising Thereunder (1972) [hereinafter referred to as HANSON], identified the first, third, and fourth approaches in analyzing state journalist statutes.

145. See, e.g., ARK. STAT. ANN. § 43-9117 (1964); MICH. STAT. ANN. § 2945(1) (1954); NEV. REV. STAT. § 49.275 (1971).

146. Drug Abuse Office and Treatment Act of 1972, 21 U.S.C. § 1175 (Supp. 1972).

147. Comprehensive Drug Abuse Prevention and Control Act of 1970, 42 U.S.C. 242a(a) (1971) and 21 U.S.C. 872(c) (1971). See also Comprehensive

Alcohol and Alcoholism Prevention, Treatment, and Rehabilitation Act of 1970, 42 U.S.C. 4582 (1971).
148. The first and third approaches can be synthesized. Coverage could extend to individuals "engaged in research." While the statute would protect all those who have access to research data, the absence of a definition of the term "research" is a source of ambiguity.
149. This approach may be best suited for a statute protecting only those individuals involved in federal evaluation research.
150. But see NEJELSKI and LERMAN, supra note 1 at 1141-42 (1971), advocating a functional approach for the coverage of a researcher privilege statute.
151. E.g., S. DOC. NO. 158, 93rd Cong., 1st Sess. (1973), disseminating news through any news media; Minnesota Free Flow of Information Act, § 3 for purpose of transmission, dissemination or publication to the public.
152. See "Relevant Statutes for Journalists" at B-21ff. supra.
153. Minnesota Free Flow of Information Act, § 3.
154. § 5(1). The term "researcher" means any person who is or was, at the time of exposure to the information or thing sought by subpoena or legal process, engaged in gathering, compiling, storing, analyzing, reviewing, editing, disseminating through any media, or publishing research data. § 5(2). The term "research data" means any information obtained (i) employing principles recognized or standards accepted in the field of inquiry (ii) for the purpose of public benefit.
155. As is pointed out in "Case Histories" at B-12ff. supra, the need for a researcher's privilege spans a wide variety of areas of inquiry, ranging from the historian involved in investigating recent history, Popkin, to the social scientist evaluating the effect of an experimental government benefits project, the New Jersey negative income tax experiment, to the medical doctor assessing the effectiveness of methadone, Doctor Newman.
156. But see Comment, Functional Overlap Between the Lawyer and Other Professionals: Its Implication For the Privileged Communications Doctrine, 71 YALE L. REV. 1226, 1257, 1260 (1962) for a discussion that psychiatrists, psychologists, and social workers perform functions that overlap with lawyers' functions.
157. Licensing journalists and, thus, researchers would result in possible prior restraint of First Amendment rights. The Court has always put a heavy burden on the proponents of such a restraint in order to justify it. New York Times v. United States, 403 U.S. 713 (1971), Bantam Books Inc. v. Sullivan, 372 U.S. 58 (1963); see also Near v. Minnesota, 283 U.S. 697 (1931).
158. Individuals with such credentials, however, would be covered by the statute without question. Cf. American Civil Liberties Union Testimonial Privilege for Researchers, Memorandum from Privacy Committee to Board of Directors, April 6, 1973 (mimeographed):

> The researcher may be employed at a school, college, university, or at a research institution, foundation, government agency or other profit or non-profit entity in which empirical research is undertaken. Independent persons without explicit employment as "researchers" may also qualify by virtue of being engaged in collecting empirical information under a qualified instructor for the purpose of satisfying some requirement for an

academic degree, or by virtue of demonstration to the
court of a bona fide interest in research and the
dissemination of information to the public.

159. This is analogous to the situation of the reporter for an underground newspaper or the freelancer in the news area. A number of shield laws are drafted so as to specifically exclude freelancers, e.g., IND. ANN. STAT. § 2-1733 (1971) extends coverage only to a person connected with a weekly, semiweekly, triweekly, or daily newspaper; H.R. DOC. NO. 2002, 93rd Cong., 1st Sess. (1973), extends coverage only to individuals who are collecting, writing, or editing news. Statutes are also drafted to exclude the underground press and other publications of narrow circulation. E.g., IND. ANN. STAT. § 2-1733 (1971) requires that the individual be connected with a newspaper that has published for five consecutive years in the same city or town and that has a paid circulation of two percent of the population of the county where it is published (amended in 1973 to be less restrictive, see 1973 PUB. L. 319; § 1, pp. 1731).

160. Cf. ACLU memorandum similarly extends coverage to all those within the research environment who have access to the information sought (collection, analysis, or reporting). See also, a number of shield laws for journalists that similarly extend coverage. E.g., S. DOC. NO. 158, 93rd Cong., 1st Sess., § 6(3) (1973).

161. Cf. Farr v. Superior Court, 22 Cal. App. 3d 60, 99 Cal. Rptr. 342 (1971) for a case interpreting the California newsman shield law so as not to protect reporters, once they have terminated their affiliation with a newspaper, from compelled disclosure of information received while reporters. This case has inspired state and federal legislators to include in proposed statutes provisions specifically protecting an individual who, while no longer a reporter, received the sought information while a reporter. See also Bridge v. New Jersey, 120 N.J. Super. 460, 295 A. 2d 3 (1972), cert. denied, 410 U.S. 991 (1973).

162. Proposed Statute, § 5(2).

163. E.g., research done by a pharmaceutical company to develop new drugs.

164. E.g., research conducted by investment analysts for their clients and market research done by a corporation in the course of defending an anti-trust case.

165. The commercial speech doctrine can be traced to Valentine v. Christensen, 316 U.S. 52, 54 (1942). "We are equally clear that the Constitution imposes no such restraint on government as respects purely commercial advertising." (The state cannot unduly regulate speech in public thoroughfares.) The Court in New York Times v. Sullivan, 376 U.S. 254 (1964), qualified the Valentine doctrine. The fact that a newspaper profited from an advertisement did not mean that speech was not protected by the First Amendment. The factor that made commercial speech unprotected was that the advertisement did no more than propose a commercial transaction. Most recently, in Pittsburgh Press Co. v. Pittsburgh Commission on Human Relations, 413 U.S. 376 (1973), the Court addressed the commercial speech doctrine. In ruling that the states can forbid newspapers from carrying sex-designated want ads, the Court stated that the advertisement came within the Valentine type situation. It neither expressed a position on the social policy of whether certain positions should be filled by one

sex and not the other nor criticized the state's prohibition of sex designated advertisement. The advertisements were thus viewed as a "classic example of commercial speech." Id. at 379.

166. See discussion of the relationship between the First Amendment and the public benefit requirements, notes 163 and 164 supra and accompanying text.

167. The greatest limitation on the protection of state shield laws for journalists results from the listing of the media covered. See HANSON, note 144 supra. E.g., N.J. STAT. ANN. 2A:84A-21 (Supp. 1969) (protection given only to individuals connected with newspapers); CAL. EVID. CODE ANN. § 1070 (West Supp. 1971) and OHIO REV. CODE ANN. § 2739.12 (1953) (protect only individuals connected with newspapers or press associations). Contra, ALAS. COMP. LAWS ANN. § 09.25.220(4)220 (1970 cum Supp.) (covers newspapers, other periodicals that report news events, newsreels, motion pictures, wire, radio, television or facsimile); Minnesota Free Flow of Information Act (no listings of media; coverage extends to all individuals who disseminate or publish information to the public).

168. See Deltec v. Dunn & Bradstreet, Inc., 187 F. Supp. 788 (N.D. Ohio 1960), stating that the Ohio shield law, OHIO REV. CODE ANN. § 2739.12 (1953), covering newspapers and press associations did not cover a Dunn & Bradstreet bi-monthly publication; Application of Cepeda, 233 F. Supp. 465 (S.D.N.Y. 1964), stating that LOOK magazine did not come within the ambit of newspapers or press associations specifically mentioned in the California statute, CAL. EVID. CODE ANN. § 1070 (West Supp. 1971).

169. § 5(1).

170. § 5(5). The term "media" means any periodical, journal, book, report, study, thesis, lecture, radio or television broadcast, cable television transmission or any other means, published or unpublished, by which research data is reported.

171. The confidentiality provisions of the Comprehensive Drug Abuse Prevention and Control Act, 42 U.S.C. § 242(a) (1971), 21 U.S.C. § 872(c) (1971), and the Comprehensive Alcohol and Alcoholism Prevention, Treatment and Rehabilitation Act, 42 U.S.C. § 4582 (1971), authorize persons "engaged in research" on drugs or alcoholism to protect the identity of "subjects of such research." Other researcher privilege statutes limit protection to records or documents maintained in connection with a specific research endeavor. See confidentiality provisions of the Drug Abuse Office and Treatment Act of 1972, 21 U.S.C. 1175 (Supp. 1972); MD. CODE ANN. art. 35 § 101 (1971) and N.Y. CIVIL RIGHTS LAW § 79-j (McKinney Supp. 1972).

172. Hearings on Newsman's Privilege, supra note 44 at 271-72 (testimony of Sanford Smith and Arthur B. Hanson) discussing the various ways in which journalist statutes limit coverage to situations when the individual is acting as a journalist. They include specifying either "an engaged in requirement" of an "in the course of a newsman's activities requirement," and granting a privilege only to information published in specified media or to information gathered for publication in specified media.

173. § 2(1) and (2). In a statute designed only to protect specific types of research, e.g., evaluation research, in the "course of federal evaluation research" could be added.

174. See "Coverage: People" at B-31ff, supra.

175. Webster's Third International Dictionary (1968). § 5(6) of the proposed Statute repeats this definition. It should be emphasized that "subjects" as defined in the proposed Statute include individuals personally observed by the researcher as well as individuals who serve to inform the researcher of their own behavior and views or the behavior and views of others. See note 201 infra for a discussion that a number of courts have interpreted news "sources" to include only individuals who act as informants to journalists as opposed to those whom the journalist personally observes.

176. Proposed Statute § 2.

177. Cf. Prof. Anthony Amsterdam, who asserts, as a justification for not requiring a promise of confidentiality in a shield statute for journalists, that it is to protect the source and not only the confidential nature of the relationship. Hearings Before the Subcomm. on Constitutional Rights of the House Comm. on the Judiciary, 93rd Cong., 1st Sess. (1973) (testimony of Anthony Amsterdam) [hereinafter referred to as TESTIMONY OF ANTHONY AMSTERDAM].

No state statute for journalists requires that the privilege be extended only when the source relationship is explicitly confidential. The statutes suggest that the communication between a reporter and informant is confidential regardless of the informant's intent. See HANSON, supra note 144 at 30. But see In re Dan, 342 N.Y.S. 2d 731, 41 A.D. 2d 687 (1973), app. dismissed, 344 N.Y.S. 2d 955, 32 N.Y. 2d 764 (1973); People v. Wolf, 69 Misc. 2d 256, 329 N.Y.S. 2d 291 (1972), aff'd per curiam, 39 App. Div. 2d 837, 333 N.Y.S. 2d 299 (1972); In re WBAI-FM, 68 Misc. 2d 355, 326 N.Y.S. 2d 434 (1971) in which the New York State courts read into the New York shield law, N.Y. CIVIL RIGHTS LAW § 79-h (McKinney 1970), a requirement of express confidentiality. Contra, Lightman v. State, 294 A. 2d 149 (Md. Ct. App. 1972), aff'd per curiam, 295 A. 2d 212, 266 Md. 550 (1972), cert. denied, 411 U.S. 951 (1973), in which, despite a possible legislative intent to only protect confidential relationships, the court viewed the Maryland statute broad enough to cover non-confidential situations. Only one group of bills presently before Congress require confidentiality for protection, H.R. 1749, 1985, 2101, 93rd Cong., 1st Sess. (1973).

178. See NEJELSKI and FINSTERBUSCH, supra note 1 at 11-12.

179. Confidentiality is to be distinguished from consent. Consent "concerns the conditions under which information is obtained from a person;" confidentiality, the conditions under which the information is used. Ruebhausen and Brim, Privacy and Behavioral Research, 65 COL. L. REV. 1184, 1197 (1965) [hereinafter referred to as RUEBHAUSEN and BRIM].

180. See generally RUEBHAUSEN and BRIM, supra note 179, for a discussion of the ethical issues of consent and confidentiality.

181. Identified in RUEBHAUSEN and BRIM, supra note 179 at 1196. The discussion on the three methodologies is largely taken from RUEBHAUSEN and BRIM.

182. E.g., researchers may be reluctant to compile candid, sensitive and personal information that may be necessary for a quality research project unless they are assured that the information will not be subject to compulsory process.

183. Cf. TESTIMONY OF ANTHONY AMSTERDAM, supra note 177 at 48. A reason for not advocating a confidentiality requirement in the area is the difficulty in defining and litigating "What is confidential?"

184. Contra, the ACLU Committee on Privacy (Memorandum to the Board of Directors on the Researcher's Privilege. April 6, 1973) believes that legislation can be drafted to reasonably provide for a court determination of the issue of whether a promise of confidentiality was expressly made or implied to the subject. The Committee, in fact, advocates that a statutory researcher's privilege extend protection only to "information collected directly from persons who have voluntarily provided such information on the basis of their reasonable expectation that their identity as participants would not be revealed and that the information they provide would not be connected with them as individuals." The Committee would so restrict the statutory coverage because it feels that if protection were available beyond such situations, any person could claim virtually any communication or observation as "confidential for the purpose of research." As a civil liberties matter, the Committee did not intend to create a privilege that could be abused by persons not serving a public information function. Contra, the proposed Statute in opting for broader coverage, assumes that some litigation may be required to determine if an individual is a bona fide researcher. (See "Coverage: People" at B-31ff. supra.) This issue can be more reliably and expediently litigated than the issue of whether a promise of confidentiality was made.

185. E.g., N.Y. CIVIL RIGHTS LAW § 79-j (McKinney Supp. 1972) (multi-state information system on psychiatric patients); MD. CODE ANN. art. 35 § 101 (1971) (State Board of Mental Health and Mental Hygiene and Maryland Commission to Study Problems of Drug Addiction); 42 U.S.C. § 242a(a) (1971) and 21 U.S.C. § 872(c) (1971) (drug abuse); 21 U.S.C. § 1175 (Supp. 1972) (drug abuse); 13 U.S.C. § 9(a) (Supp. 1972) (census information).

186. See HANSON, supra note 124 at 24. All state journalist privilege laws protect the identity of the source. But see MICH. COMP. LAWS ANN. § 767.5a (1968), which can be viewed as ambiguous on this subject, extending coverage to "communications between reporters . . . and their informants."

187. E.g., studies done by Professor Popkin on the Vietnam war and research pursued by Ralph Nader for his book, UNSAFE AT ANY SPEED (1965).

188. Note, the Public Scholar and the First Amendment: A Compelling Need for Compelling Testimony?, 40 GEO. WASH. L. REV. 995, 1010-11 (1972). See also Hearings on Freedom of the Press Before Subcomm. on Constitutional Rights of the Senate Comm. on the Judiciary, 92nd Cong., 1st and 2d Sess. (1971), [hereinafter referred to as 1971 SENATE HEARINGS], testimony of Richard Barnet at 68: "[M]odern society has become so complex and the pace of events so swift that the crucial task of keeping the public informed on vital issues cannot be performed by journalists alone . . . investigations by public scholars . . . are filling the gap left by the decline of daily investigative journalists."

189. See BLASI REPORT, supra note 19, for an empirical discussion of the effect of press subpoenas calling for reporters to reveal the identity of their sources.

190. 1971 SENATE HEARINGS, supra note 188 (testimony of Richard Barnet).

191. E.g., the decennial census, a research endeavor mandated by the United States Constitution art. I., sec. 2, cl. 3, requires all citizens to furnish various types of personal information; Gallup and Harris polls call for individuals to supply information on various special and political views; studies by the Kinsey Institute ask people to respond to questions relating to their sexual practices; researchers are contracted by the federal and state governments to obtain information from individuals on their experience as beneficiaries of social welfare programs.

192. E.g., in the New Jersey negative income tax experiment evaluation researchers elicited information to evaluate the impact of a negative income tax system of welfare. State prosecutors subpoenaed the information to determine which participants in the experiment were illegally receiving state welfare payments as well.

193. This is especially true of observing criminal activity and deviant behavior.

194. See RUEBHAUSEN and BRIM, supra note 179 at 1200, for a discussion that anonymity serves to keep invasion of the subject's privacy to a minimum, although it is not a complete answer to the ethical issue of requiring informed consent before a subject responds.

195. Certain research designs can provide for complete anonymity of subjects. This is especially true of research that involves eliciting the opinions of individuals on various social or political issues on a one-shot basis. The longitudinal study that focuses upon the growth and change of individuals over time, however, requires that individuals be resurveyed and the responses of each individual subject be kept segregated. This research is particularly vulnerable to the subpoena. A more complex method of protecting the identity of subjects was thus needed. The Link File System was developed by the American Council on Education. The system generally utilizes three files. One contains the subject's responses with an arbitrary identification number. A second file contains the names and addresses of the subjects with another set of arbitrary numbers. The third "link" file contains two sets of numbers, matching the subject response file with the name and address file. The link file is stored in a foreign country so that the researcher can in good faith resist a subpoena. See A. Astin and R. Boruch, A "Link" System For Assuring Confidentiality of Research Data in Longitudinal Studies (5 ACE Research Rep. No. 3, 1970).

196. The survey method and the longitudinal study that can preserve the anonymity of individuals are not useful in many types of research. These methods are particularly inappropriate to studies of criminal and deviant behavior, which often require personal interviews and observation. The subject's identity, thus, cannot be concealed from the researcher. The type of information accumulated in such studies can be of obvious use to law enforcement agencies possessing the power of compulsory process.

197. The Census Act provides for the greatest coverage of information received in the course of a researcher-source relationship. 13 U.S.C. § 9(a)(1) prohibits use of information received in the course of gathering census data for purposes other than the statistical purposes for which it was supplied. The confidentiality provision of the Drug Abuse Office and Treatment Act of 1972, 21 U.S.C. § 1175(a) (Supp. 1972), protects the records of the prognosis or treatment of any patient involved in drug research. Contra, the confidentiality provisions of the Comprehensive Drug Abuse Prevention and Control Act of 1972, 42 U.S.C. § 242a(a) (1971) and 21 U.S.C. § 872(c) (1971), as well as the analogous provision in the Compre-

hensive Alcohol and Alcoholism Prevention, Treatment and Rehabilitation Act of 1970, 42 U.S.C. § 4582 (1971) extends coverage only to the identity of subjects. These statutes are, however, the broadest researcher privilege laws yet enacted, for they provide absolute protection.

198. Only two existing state privilege laws for journalists extend coverage to the contents of information received from a source. The Michigan statute, MICH. STAT. ANN. § 28.94J(1) (1954), protects "communications" between reporters and their sources. The New York statute, N.Y. CIVIL RIGHTS LAW § 79-h (McKinney 1970), protects "news or the source of any such news." A number of proposed federal bills extend coverage to information received. E.g., S. DOC. NO. 158, 93rd Cong., 1st Sess. (1973), covers "information" broadly defined. H.R. DOC. NO. 3482, 93rd Cong., 1st Sess. (1973), covers "information" broadly defined.

199. Branzburg v. Pound, 461 S.W. 2d 345 (Ky. 1971), aff'd sub nom., Branzburg v. Hayes, 408 U.S. 608 (1972).

200. KY. REV. STAT. § 421.100 (1952).

201. See also Lightman v. State, 294 A. 2d 149 (Md. Ct. App. 1972), aff'd. per curiam, 295 A. 2d 212, 266 Md. 550 (1972), cert. denied, 411 U.S. 951 (1973). Lightman, a reporter who had written a story on his observation of occurrences relating to drugs at a pipe shop, was subpoenaed by a grand jury to reveal the identity of the shopkeeper. The reporter refused, claiming that the shopkeeper was the source of his information and was, thus, protected by the Maryland newsman privilege statute, MD. CODE ANN. art. 35 § 2 (1971) (protecting "the source of any news or information procured or obtained by him [the reporter] and published in the newspaper"). The court interpreted the statute so as not to protect the information obtained by Lightman because it was obtained through personal observation of the shopkeeper's illegal activity rather than through an informant whose identity would be protected by the statute.

202. § 2(1). See note 171 supra.

203. 329 U.S. 495 (1947).

204. Id. at 511.

205. Minnesota Free Flow of Information Act § 3 prohibits compelled disclosure of "any unpublished information procured . . . or any . . . notes, memoranda, recordings, tapes, films or other reportorial data which would serve to identify the person or means through which the information was obtained."

206. E.g., H.R. DOC NO. 1813, § 4(3)-(5); H.R. DOC. NO. 2187, § 4(3)-(5); H.R. DOC NO. 2200 § 4(3)-(5), 93rd Cong., 1st Sess. (1973). (These bills protect from compelled disclosure information "not disseminated to the public by the person from whom disclosure is sought . . . includ[ing] notes, outtakes, photographs, tapes or other data of whatever sort not itself disseminated to the public . . .")

207. Proposed Statute, § 5(2) and (3).

208. FED. R. CRIM. P. 16.

209. FED. R. CIV. P. 26.

210. 408 U.S. at 709.

211. Proposed Statute, § 2.

212. Contra, a few existing researcher statutes explicitly restrict coverage to specifically mentioned types of data, e.g., patient records. See

"Statutes: Existing and Proposed" at B-19ff, supra for a discussion of such statutes: 21 U.S.C. § 1175 (Supp. 1972), N.Y. CIVIL RIGHTS LAW § 79-j (McKinney 1972), and MD. CODE ANN. art. 35 § 101 (1971).

213. Contra, a number of proposed statutes for journalists before the 93rd Congress define the term "information" so as to preclude limiting coverage to specific ways in which information is stored. E.g., S. DOC. NO. 158, 93rd Cong., 1st Sess. (1973); H.R. DOC. NO. 1813 § 4(3)-(5); H.R. DOC. NO. 2187, § 4(3)-(5); H.R. DOC. NO. 2200 § 4(3)-(5), 93rd Cong., 1st Sess. (1973).

214. Proposed Statute, § 5(5).

215. See following discussion rejecting the absolute-qualified dichotomy often used to describe privilege conferring statutes.

216. See generally McCormick, EVIDENCE (1954) [hereinafter referred to as McCORMICK], § 91 at 187-91 (presence of a third party); § 95 at 194-200 (consultation in furtherance of Crime of Fraud).

217. 68 Misc. 2d 355, 326 N.Y.S. 2d 434 (1971). See also Baker v. F & F Investment, 339 F. Supp. 942 (S.D.N.Y. 1972), where a federal district court stated that in interpreting the New York newsman privilege statute, N.Y. CIVIL RIGHTS LAW § 79-h, no exceptions were consistent with the policy of the Illinois newsman statute. The Illinois statute provides an exception to the privilege in actions for defamation and that the privilege may be denied if all other sources of information have been exhausted and disclosure is essential to the public interest.

218. N.Y. CIVIL RIGHTS LAW § 79-h (McKinney 1972).

219. 21 U.S.C. § 1175 (Supp. 1972).

220. 21 U.S.C. § 1175(b)(c) (Supp. 1972).

221. E.g., N.M. STAT. ANN. § 20-1-12.1 (Supp. 1970) considers the following factors in determining whether or not a privilege should be granted: (1) the nature of the proceeding; (2) the merits of the claim or defense; (3) the adequacy of the remedy otherwise available, if any; (4) the possibility of establishing by other means that which it is alleged the source requested will tend to prove.

222. See "Current Judicial Protection" at B-16ff. supra.

223. See NEJELSKI and LERMAN, supra note 1 at 1087-89.

224. The power of the grand jury to compel testimony has been consistently recognized by the U.S. Supreme Court. See Branzburg v. Hayes, 408 U.S. 665, 688 (1972), citing Blair v. United States, 250 U.S. 273 (1919), for the proposition that the grand jury's authority to subpoena witnesses is historic, 250 U.S. at 279-81. The Branzburg court regarded the power as "essential." 408 U.S. at 688.

225. The power of congressional committees to compel testimony was recognized by the U.S. Supreme Court in Watkins v. United States, 354 U.S. 178 (1957). Furthermore, the power can be enforced by Congress pursuant to the contempt of Congress statute, 2 U.S.C. § 192 (1970).

226. On the federal level, Congress has passed legislation granting the power of compulsory process to a variety of administrative agencies. E.g., 15 U.S.C. § 1312(a) (1970), (Anti-Trust Division of the Department of Justice); 47 U.S.C. § 409(e) (1970), (F.C.C.); 29 U.S.C. § 161 (1970), (N.L.R.B.).

227. Defendants in criminal trials have a constitutional right to compel

testimony, U.S. CONST. amend. VI; FED. R. CRIM. P. 17(e) (1973). Prosecutors, as well, have the power to compel testimony, FED. R. CRIM. P. 17(e).

228. E.g., FED. R. CIV. P. 4(e) provides civil litigants in federal court the power of compulsory process, though limited by a territorial restriction of 100 miles. However, the power of civil litigants to compel testimony is not constitutionally mandated.

229. E.g., the Drug Abuse Prevention and Control Act of 1970 and the Comprehensive Alcohol and Alcoholism Prevention, Treatment and Rehabilitation Act of 1970 confer protection to researchers in "civil, criminal, legislative or other proceedings;" the A.C.L.U. Privacy Committee Memorandum on a Testimonial Privilege for Researchers (April 6, 1973, mimeographed) also confers protection to a researcher "in any court, legislative or other body having the contempt power."

230. E.g., N.Y. CIVIL RIGHTS LAW § 79-j (McKinney Supp. 1972) makes records of the multi-state information system for psychiatric patients "not subject to examination in the court or by agencies of this [N.Y.] state." In the news area, the "general" statutes do not mention specific proceedings, only specifying the dimensions of the privilege. E.g., MD. CODE ANN. art. 35 § 2 (1971); MICH. STAT. ANN. § 38.945(1) (1954); N.J. STAT. ANN. 2A:84A-21 (Supp. 1969). The New Jersey court has held that the New Jersey statute can be asserted at discovery, as well as at trial, despite the fact that specific proceedings are not listed. Beecroft v. Point Pleasant Printing & Publishing Co., 82 N.J. Super. 259, 197 A. 2d 416 (1964).

231. Professor Vince Blasi, drafter for the National Conference of Commissioners on Uniform State Laws of the Uniform Information Source Protection Act, is the main proponent of this approach in the news area. A uniform law has not yet been approved by the Commissioners on Uniform State Laws. The statute is still in draft form, the latest draft being that of April 1, 1973.

232. The April 1973 draft defines adjudicative proceedings as "any proceeding in which a judicially enforceable final judgment may be rendered, but does not include any proceeding of a grand jury or any other accusatorial or investigative proceeding." See generally Hearings on H.R. 717, Before Subcomm. No. 3 of the House Comm. on the Judiciary, 93rd Cong., 1st Sess. 1611 (1973) (statement of Vince Blasi) [hereinafter referred to as STATEMENT OF BLASI].

233. Id. at 142-43.
234. Id. at 143.
235. Id. at 142-43.
236. Testimony of Professor Vince Blasi at ABA Committee Newsman Shield Law Hearings, June 10, 1973. Rather than advocating specific qualifications, Professor Blasi proposed a flexible standard by which a court would balance the need for the contents of the source communication with the detriment to the journalist.
237. Proposed Statute, § 2.
238. ALAS. COMP. LAWS ANN. § 09.24.160(b) (Supp. 1970). The court may deny the privilege if it "results in a miscarriage of justice."
239. S. DOC. NO. 1311, 92nd Cong., 1st Sess. (1972), provides an exception for threat to human life or espionage. See also H.R. DOC. NO. 2101,

93rd Cong., 1st Sess. § 4 (1973). Another group of proposed statutes provides for an exception to the privilege if the following tripartite test is met: (1) there is a probable cause that the protected person has information clearly relevant to a specific probable violation; (2) the information cannot be obtained by alternative means; and (3) there is a compelling and overriding national interest in the information. E.g., H.R. DOC. NO. 265, 93rd Cong., 1st Sess. § 3 (1973). This reflects the test suggested by a number of the petitioners in the Branzburg v. Hayes litigation as well as the view taken by Justice Stewart dissenting in Branzburg, 408 U.S. at 743.

240. 408 U.S. at 690-91.
241. Testimony of Robert Dixon, Senate Hearings on Newsmen's Privilege, supra note 44.
242. Thirteen of the 19 state journalist statutes do not set forth any qualifications for law enforcement purposes. None of the researcher statutes specifically make an exception for law enforcement purposes.
243. See "Case Histories" at B-12ff. supra.
244. E.g., H.R. DOC. NO. 3369, 93rd Cong., 1st Sess. (1973). See note 239 supra.
245. Exceptions to the confidentiality provisions of the Social Security Act are made in cases of national security and for information concerning aliens as requested by the Attorney General under § 209(c) of the Immigration and Nationality Act of 1952, 8 U.S.C. 1360(c) (1970).
246. See Korematsu v. United States, 323 U.S. 214 (1945), in which the Court justified the internment of Japanese aliens on the West Coast for national security purposes.
247. Draft Report of the President's Commission on Federal Statistics, U.S. Government Printing Office, Wash., D.C. Vol. II (1971).
248. See BLASI REPORT, note 19 supra at 247.
249. E.g., drug use, possession, and sale; prostitution; gambling; sexual deviance; pornography use, possession and sale; and generally all crimes that principally harm the individual involved rather than society at large. Many prominent criminologists, in fact, advocate decriminalizing this type of activity. See generally BLASI REPORT, note 19 supra, citing H. Packer, THE LIMITS OF CRIMINAL SANCTIONS (1969); N. Morris & G. Hawkins, THE HONEST POLITICIAN'S GUIDE TO CRIME CONTROL (1970); J. Kaplan, MARIJUANA--THE NEW PROHIBITION (1971).
250. It is convenient to include in "political corruption" criminal activity that involves recipients of public benefit programs usurping their rights under the program, information likely to be revealed in the course of research to evaluate the public benefit programs.
251. Letter to the authors from George Van Hoomissen, March 3, 1971, quoted in NEJELSKI and LERMAN, supra note 1 at 1101 n. 64. Cf. House Hearings, supra note 42 at 453 (testimony of Hon. William Cahn, District Attorney for Nassau County, N.Y., and immediate past president of the National District Attorneys Association, testifying on newsman's privilege).

> But whatever the extent of the suppressive effect, [from compelling newsman to testify] if the content of news and its depth and quality are thus diminished or impaired in the short range interest of law enforcement, the ultimate result may be long range disadvantage

to law enforcement and social health.
252. H.R. DOC. NO. 3369, 93rd Cong., 1st Sess. § 7(c)(3) (1973), provides an exception to the privilege in proceedings involving "murder, forcible rape, aggravated assault, kidnapping, and airline hijacking or when a breach of national security has been established . . . In no case, however, shall the application [for an exception] be granted where the crime at issue is corruption or malfeasance in office." See also Hearings on Newsmen's Privilege, note 18 supra (testimony of William Cahn) at 453 and BLASI REPORT, note 19 supra at 251.
253. The researcher studying criminal behavior in this way may use unethical practices to elicit incriminating responses from subjects, for example, by paying the subject for candid responses. Because the statute is designed in part to protect the subject's privacy interest, it should serve to offset the unethical behavior of the researcher in eliciting the information by allowing the researcher to resist compelled disclosure of the information.
254. See "Case Histories" at B-12ff, supra.
255. 42 U.S.C. § 242a(a) (1970); 21 U.S.C. § 872(c) (1970).
256. Knowledge of future drug transactions is, as well, knowledge of crimes to be committed in the future. A number of old cases limited the future crimes exception of the attorney-client privilege to intended crimes involving "malum in se" or moral turpitude. See McCORMICK, note 216 supra, § 199 at 200 n. 56 citing Bank of Utica v. Mesereau, 3 Barb. On. 528, 598 (1848); Hughes v. Boone, 102 N.C. 137, 9 S.E. 286, 292 (1899). Modern authorities, however, view such a limitation as inappropriate because the exception to the privilege merely has the consequence of opening the door to the evidence at trial. McCORMICK § 199 at 201.
257. But consider that the common law historically recognized a duty to report felonies. It prescribed criminal liability for failure to do so under the crime of "misprison of a felony." Convictions for such an offense, however, were rare. F. Perkins, CRIMINAL LAW, 512 (2d ed. 1969). While today it is questionable whether a citizen has a legal affirmative duty to report a crime, the Supreme Court has stated that "concealment of crime and agreements to do so are not looked upon with favor." Branzburg, 408 U.S. at 697. Morality may, however, dictate that the researcher reveal future crimes to law enforcement authorities. This may be done whether or not a privilege exists.
258. Cf. the psychotherapist- or psychiatrist-patient privilege, argued to be analogous to the researcher-subject privilege, for both depend on developing a working relationship with the respondent. NEJELSKI and LERMAN, supra note 1 at 1146. State legislatures have not agreed on whether to divest this privilege in the context of future crimes. The Connecticut legislature consciously did not provide a future crimes exception. Goldstein & Katz, Psychiatrist-Patient Privilege: The GAP Proposal and the Connecticut Statute, 118 AM. J. PSYCHIATRY 733, 738-39 (1962). Contra, MASS. ANN. LAWS Ch. 233 § 20B (1969) making an exception to the psychotherapist-patient privilege where the psychotherapist believes a present "threat of imminently dangerous activity" by the patient towards himself or herself or others.
259. The Sixth Amendment compulsory process applies equally in federal and state proceedings. Washington v. Texas, 388 U.S. 14 (1967).

260. 388 U.S. at 19.
261. See generally J. Brennan, <u>The Criminal Prosecution: Sporting Event or Quest for Truth?</u> 1963 WASH. U.L.Q. 279, 285-88 (1963).
262. Rule 17(d) of the Federal Rules of Criminal Procedure was amended in 1966 to make it less difficult for poor defendants to subpoena witnesses, providing for court payment of subpoena fees upon defendant's showing of "inability to pay" rather than "indigency." The revisions also make the defendant's application for subpoena fees an <u>ex parte</u> proceeding so that the application would not serve to provide strategic information for the prosecution. The 1966 revision also decreases the defendant's burden of proof for the issuance of a subpoena from materiality of the testimony to necessity to prepare an adequate defense. Finally, upon an adequate showing by the defense the new rule provides that the court "shall" rather than "may" issue a subpoena.
263. <u>Branzburg v. Hayes</u>, 408 U.S. at 705.
264. <u>State v. Groppi</u>, 164 N.W. 2d 266, 271, 41 Wis. 2d 312 (1969), <u>rev'd on other grounds</u>, 400 U.S. 505 (1971). The court rejected the attempt of Father Groppi to subpoena witnesses.
265. <u>United States v. Beye</u>, 445 F. 2d 1037 (9th Cir. 1971).
266. 354 F. Supp. 208 (D.D.C. 1972). See "Current Judicial Protection" at B-16ff. supra and note 107 supra.
267. 354 F. Supp. at 216.
268. Id. at 216.
269. Id. at 215.
270. Adopted from H.R. DOC. NO. 2651, 93rd Cong., 1st Sess. § 3 (1973).
271. <u>Branzburg v. Hayes</u>, 408 U.S. at 690.
272. See "Current Judicial Protection" at B-16ff. supra discussing <u>Baker v. F & F Investment</u> and <u>Democratic National Committee v. McCord</u>, note 40 supra and accompanying text.
273. Contra, see "Statutes: Existing and Proposed" at B-19ff. supra, which provide for judicial balancing. These statutes make it possible for courts on a case-by-case method to accommodate law enforcement interests by divesting the privilege when necessary.
274. See <u>Hearings on Newsman's Privilege</u>, note 44 supra (testimony of Sanford Smith and Arthur B. Hanson) at 262, stating that about half of the qualified journalist privilege bills presently before the 93rd Congress provide such an exception.
275. E.g., Minnesota Free Flow of Information Act.
276. 376 U.S. 254 (1964).
277. In ordinary libel cases, the defendant has the burden of proof to show the truth of the published story. The defendant, therefore, has the choice of either revealing the source or protecting the source and thereby risking an adverse judgment if truth can be proven in no other way. See <u>Note, Reporters and their Sources: The Constitutional Right to a Confidential Relationship</u>, 80 YALE L. J. 317 (1970).
278. 376 U.S. at 279-80. The Court, thus, shifted the burden of proof as well as the burden of coming forward to the plaintiff in libel actions. Defendants in libel actions under the <u>New York Times</u> rule are stripped of the traditional presumption of malice against them as well as the necessity of proving an affirmative defense of truth. This was done to foster the First Amendment interest in brisk public discourse.

279. 390 U.S. 727 (1968).
280. 390 U.S at 731.
281. "A defamatory communication usually has been defined as one which tends to hold the plaintiff up to hatred, contempt or ridicule or to cause him to be shunned or ridiculed." Prosser, LAW OF TORTS (4th ed. 1971) [hereinafter referred to as PROSSER] § 111 at 739.
282. Recoveries against the press, however, have been made. See Goldwater v. Ginzberg, 414 F. 2d 324 (2d Cir. 1969), cert. denied, 396 U.S. 1049 (1970), reh. denied, 397 U.S. 978 (1970).
283. In addition to any living person, business entities can also be defamed. While a corporation, a partnership, etc., has no personal reputation, it does have "standing" and "prestige" in the business community, and language which disparages its reputation may be actionable. PROSSER, supra note 281, § 111 at 745.
284. A communication to a third party is essential for an action for defamation. The technical term for this is "publication" though there is no requirement that the material be published in the conventional sense. PROSSER, supra note 281, § 113 at 766.
285. 17 Cal. App. 3d 621, 95 Cal. Rptr. 175 (1971). See also B. Thorton, White v. State of California and Code Sections 11120-11127: A Pre-Computer Privacy Case and the Legislative "Answer." 47 L.A. BAR J. 320 (1972).
286. CA. CIV. CODE § 47 (1954).
287. Actual malice is defined as "that state of mind arising from hatred or ill will toward the plaintiff." CA. CIV. CODE § 48(a)(4) (1954).
288. A number of absolute privileges have been established immunizing certain communications from any defamation action. E.g., statements made in the course of judicial proceedings; communications of executive officers of the government. See also Justice Black concurring in Rosenbloom v. Metromedia, 403 U.S. 29 (1971), stating that the First Amendment does not permit recovery of libel judgments against the news media under any circumstances.
289. Perhaps the best generalization is that a communication is so protected if it was "fairly made by a person in the discharge of some public or **private duty,** whether legal or moral, or in the context of his own affairs in the matters where his interest is concerned." Toogood v. Sprying, 1 C.M. & R. 181, 149 Eng. Rep. 1044 (1834), quoted in PROSSER, supra note 281, § 115 at 786. For a general discussion of communications so protected, see sources cited in PROSSER, supra note 281, § 115 at 786 n. 75.
290. See PROSSER, supra note 281, § 115 at 791 n. 41.
291. Id. at 792.
292. E.g., Carey v. Hume, Senate Hearings on Newsmen's Privilege, note 44 supra.
293. See Cervantes v. Time Inc., 464 F. 2d 986 (8th Cir. 1972), cert. denied, 409 U.S. 1125 (1973).
294. Taken from Minnesota Free Flow of Information Act § 4.
295. See NEJELSKI and FINSTERBUSCH, note 1 supra at 14 in which a hypothetical is furnished to point out the potential conflict. A teachers union sues the Office of Education in order to obtain the raw data from a study of contract teaching. The basic analysis had not been compiled by the Office of Education. The teacher's union argues that it should have an opportunity to evaluate the data compiled, for its members will be

adversely affected by results revealing that innovative teaching methods are better than those traditionally used.

296. 44 U.S.C. § 3501 et seq. (1970).
297. 5 U.S.C. § 552 (1970).
298. 14 U.S.C. § 3507 (1970).
299. 44 U.S.C. § 3508(b) (1970).
300. The Act requires that federal agencies make available to the public in the Federal Register information about their organizational structures, operating methods and procedures, rules, policies and interpretations. Also available to the public for copying are the agencies' final adjudicatory decisions, precedents, staff manuals that affect the public, and indices for all matters required to be published. These requirements are conformed by a rule that agencies cannot rely on the above information unless it is indexed and published or made available to the public.
301. This exemption could be interpreted to prohibit disclosure of information made confidential by a federal researcher's privilege statute. On the other hand, the provision is more likely to be applied to exempt from the Act only data that are <u>specifically</u> exempt rather than data exempt by a general researcher's privilege.
302. 301 F. Supp. 796 (S.D.N.Y. 1969), <u>dismissed as moot</u>, 436 F. 2d 1363 (2d Cir. 1971).
303. The court reasoned that confidentiality was not assured because the requests stated that the information could not be withheld from other federal agencies. The other federal agencies could then release the information to the public.
304. Note that the disclosure obligation applies only to federal research. See Nathanson, <u>Social Science and Administrative Law and the Information Act of 1966</u>, 21 SOC. PROBS. 21 (1973), for a discussion of the availability of information to the researcher through the Freedom of Information Act.
305. See, e.g., <u>Getman v. National Labor Relations Board</u>, 450 F. 2d 670 (D.C. Cir. 1971). (Two labor law professors and a psychology professor were granted access to names and addresses of employees eligible to unite in a union election in the possession of the N.L.R.B. These researchers were studying the impact of campaign techniques on the union election.)
306. But see Davis, ADMINISTRATIVE LAW TREATISE (1972), concluding that even if the Freedom of Information Act were "fully obeyed, the information that the Act opens up that would otherwise be closed is minimal."
307. See <u>Consumers Union of United States v. Veterans Administration</u>, 301 F. Supp. at 806-08, stating that suits to compel disclosure under the Freedom of Information Act are in equity and, thus, the ultimate decision will be based on balancing the competing interests of privacy and the public's right to know.
308. Proposed Statute § 2(1) and (2).
309. Proposed Statute § 5(1).
310. But consider the procedures in obtaining a grant of confidentiality under the Drug Abuse Prevention and Treatment Act of 1970, which requires that researchers get approval from the Department of Health, Education, and Welfare that they are involved in bona fide drug research. This effectively means that researchers must sustain the burden of proof.

311. ARK. STAT. ANN. § 43-917 (1964) seems to place the burden upon the person seeking the information.
312. See "Coverage: People" at B-31ff, supra.
313. In order to divest the privilege the government must "(1) show that there is probable cause to believe that the newsman has information that is clearly relevant to a specific probable violation of the law; (2) demonstrate that the information sought cannot be obtained by alternative means less destructive of First Amendment rights; and (3) demonstrate a compelling and overriding interest in the information." 408 U.S. at 743.
314. 21 U.S.C. § 1175(b)(2) (Supp. 1974).
315. E.g., NEV. REV. STAT. § 49.385 (1971); N.J. STAT. ANN. 2A:84A-21 (Supp. 1969).
316. N.Y. CIVIL RIGHTS LAW § 79-h (McKinney 1971).
317. 69 Misc. 2d 256, 329 N.Y.S. 2d 291 (1972), aff'd. per curiam, 39 App. Div. 2d 837, 333 N.Y.S. 2d 299 (1972). In affirming the Supreme Court, the Appellate Division implied that the reporter's case would have been improved if he had shown that the manuscript contained information that was deleted from the article.
318. 342 N.Y.S. 2d 731, 41 A.D. 2d 687 (1973), app. dismissed, 344 N.Y.S. 2d 955, 32 N.Y. 2d 764 (1973).
319. See also Application of Howard 136 Cal. App. 2d 816, 289 P. 2d 537 (3rd Dist. 1955) and In re Taylor, 412 Pa. 32, 193 A. 2d 181 (1963). While both the California and the Pennsylvania journalist privilege statutes do not contain waiver provisions, both cases indicate that waiver will be implied when statements of the informer are publicly disclosed or published.
320. § 3: Waiver.
321. McCORMICK, supra note 216, § 93 at 194.
322. Id. at 218.
323. See note 216 supra. See also BLASI REPORT, note 19 supra at 285-89, discussing arguments for the subject to control the privilege but concluding that the arguments in favor of the journalist controlling the privilege are stronger. Contra, Note, Reporters and Their Sources: The Constitutional Right to a Confidential Relationship, 80 YALE L.J. 317, 369-70 (1970).
324. Other parties, however, have a stake in the privilege. See "Introduction" at B-1ff. supra.
325. Accord, NEJELSKI and LERMAN, supra note 1 at 1145.
326. E.g., observational or survey techniques.
327. This provision does not, however, apply if the researcher knows the subject's identity but agrees not to reveal it.
328. Contra, People v. Wolf, supra note 317. Publication of a stay in the Village Voice was held to effectively waive the protection conferred in the New York privilege.
329. See, e.g., McCORMICK, note 216 supra, § 91 at 187-92 (attorney-client) and § 101 at 216-18 (doctor-patient).